Praise for *Reframin...*

Christine is a voice I trust. This book
and deep scriptural guidance in the one gift that fused with Love could
strengthen every believer to live lives of passionate beauty. What's on offer
is a way to open the eyes of our heart - the only kind of seeing that really
matters eternally. I'm so grateful.

—**Danielle Strickland,** justice advocate,
founder, Boundless Communications, Inc.,
author of *The Other Side of Hope,*
The Ultimate Exodus, and Better Together

There is a great need within the charismatic church for a more mature
approach to the use of spiritual gifts, especially prophecy. In this book,
Christine Westhoff addresses this need, offering a wise, mature, biblically
grounded guide to the practice of prophecy in various contexts. I recommend this book for those wanting to grow in prophecy themselves and
those who wish to pastor this gift more effectively.

—**Dr. Lucy Peppiatt,**
principal, WTC Theology, UK,
author of *The Imago Dei: Humanity Made in the Image of God,*
Rediscovering Scripture's Vision for Women,
Unveiling Paul's Women, and Women and Worship at Corinth

i

Christine Westhoff is a remarkable leader. She has a tried and tested prophetic ministry, a gift of leadership, and a passion to see the prophetic ministry take its place alongside other ministries in releasing the church into its true destiny. This book is the fruit of this ministry and leadership. It models her passion for scripture and her quest to draw on quality biblical scholarship and is an excellent resource for those wanting to explore the prophetic gift, both from an individual angle and also the lens of Church leadership.

—Roger Ellis,
International Team Leader,
24-7 Prayer Community Networks,
Leadership Revelation Church
Chichester, UK

Christine Westhoff is a challenging and important prophetic voice in the Church. One that keeps aligning the people of God towards Jesus. One that has stayed normal. One that has become a trusted friend. I have profited from and I strongly recommend her teaching.

—Dr. Maximilian Oettingen, director,
Loretto Community Catholic Church,
German speaking world

Christine Westhoff is a gift to the church. Her years of service and ministry have seasoned her voice; her book offers a valuable, authentic, and honest contribution to anyone seeking to understand the role and practice of the prophetic gift within the body of Christ today. Christine communicates with clarity, grace and wisdom to illuminate a complex and at times puzzling gift, and in doing so, inspires a hope filled desire to apply the teachings of this book in your own life.

—**Brian Heasley,** director,
International Prayer, 24-7 Prayer,
author of *Be Still: A Simple
Guide to Quiet Times, and Gatecrashing*

ReFraming the Prophetic

REFRAMING THE PROPHETIC

ReFraming the Prophetic

REFRAMING THE PROPHETIC

A Biblical Observation of an Ancient Gift

Christine Westhoff

Foreword by Pete Greig

hawkeye.pro

Reframing The Prophetic

Copyright © 2024 by Christine Westhoff

Published by Hawkeye.pro
Nashville, Tennessee

ISBN 13: 978-0-9965621-7-1 (Hardback)
ISBN 13: 978-0-9965621-6-4 (Paperback)
ISBN 13: 978-0-9965621-8-8 (eBook)

Unless otherwise noted, all Scriptre quotations taken from the New American Standard Bible, © Copyright 1960, 1962, 1963, 1968, 1971, 1972, 1973, 1975, 1977, 1995 by The Lockman Foundation. Used by permission.

Emphases in Scripture quotations have been added by the author.

Printed in the United States of America

10 9 8 7 6 5 4 3 2 1 KDP 28 27 26 25 24

Contents

ReFraming the Prophetic

Acknowledgments

Special thanks to all who have labored with me, in various ways and over many years, to bring this book into being. You know who you are! A special thank you to Lori Janke, my writing coach, editor, and good friend. You have been my midwife in every way. Without you, I would have given up many times over.

ReFraming the Prophetic

Foreword

I had three precious days alone in a cottage near the ocean to work without distraction on a book long overdue with my publishers. It was to be extraordinarily precious time - costly for my team back in the office, and for Sammy, picking up the load at home with the kids. In fact, as I said goodbye to one of our sons he asked how much I expected to write while I was away and I foolishly replied 'two or three chapters'.

Upon arriving I unpacked, stocked the fridge with a few basic provisions, spread my reference books across the kitchen table, and opened my laptop. But then, suddenly overwhelmed with tiredness, I decided to take a short nap. Several hours later I woke up on the sofa with a start. Dusk was falling so I decided to wake myself up for a more productive evening by heading out immediately for a run before it got completely dark. This run led to a shower, and the shower led to supper, and the supper led to a cup of coffee sitting back down on the sofa to gather my thoughts.

And that was when God spoke. At least, I think he spoke. It wasn't audible; wasn't undeniable, but it seemed to come with a familiar weight: "Lie down." The tone was forceful. It wasn't a polite invitation to recline, but rather the kind of command you might give to your dog: "Lie. Down!"

And so, of course, I did. I lay back down on that sofa and stayed there quite happily until bedtime. Day one of my precious writing retreat had been and gone and I hadn't written a single thing. Not a chapter, not a paragraph, not a word.

The next day was also spent obediently lying on that sofa. And so was day three. In fact my diligent reclining was interrupted only by mealtimes, the occasional run, and a short walk to bed. It was on one of these runs that the Lord showed me an orchard in which the fruit had ripened at different speeds. He began to speak to me about passing on the leadership of the various ministries I'd started: first, the Order of the Mustard Seed, next the organisation behind 24-7 Prayer, and third, Emmaus Rd Church. Looking back it was an extraordinarily significant moment of strategic redirection with massive repercussions for many (and I'm pleased to report that all three organisations continue to thrive under new executive leadership teams.)

But here's the thing: I'm actually not very good at discerning God's voice. I often get it wrong. Without the benefit of hindsight I couldn't be completely sure that it really, truly had been the Lord telling me to lie down. It was entirely possible that I had merely been lazy, wasting three precious days of writing at other people's expense, and now trying to justify it spiritually. What on earth was I going to say to Sammy when I got home, and to our son when he asked, as he surely would, if I'd managed to write those three chapters?

I was worrying about this, fighting a losing battle against feelings of shame, as I packed my bag to head home, when my phone went ping. An audio message from someone on the other side of the world, 4,500 miles west, and six hours behind me. Chris Westhoff's familiar voice: "Pete, are you okay? What's going on? I was praying for you and I saw you lying down. Prostrate. I couldn't tell if you were resting or praying. There were clouds of locusts above you. But as you remained prostrate they just cleared away. The Lord wants to tell you that rest is a weapon. Lie down and you'll get clarity and see victory."

I gasped and thanked God. My faithful friend far away in Tulsa, Oklahoma had brought the word of the Lord directly into my life at exactly the right time with extraordinary accuracy in ways she could not possibly have humanly known.

Mark Twain is attributed with saying: "Some people are troubled by the things in the Bible they can't understand, but I'm troubled by the things I can understand." Our problem with God's Word, written or spoken, is often how straightforward it can be. One little-known example is a startling verse in the book of Deuteronomy which says very simply that: 'When a prophet speaks in the name of the Lord, if the word does not come to pass or come true, that is a word that the Lord has not spoken.' (Deut. 18:22)

Isn't this refreshingly practical? If a prophecy is from the Lord it will 'come to pass' if it's predictive, or 'come true' if it's formative. One way or another genuine prophecies will bear fruit eventually (generally much more slowly than we want or expect). There's a reassuring pragmatism here with regard to the one who prophecies. Clearly, even in Bible times, such people weren't expected to get it right all the time. And so, in our own time, it's still appropriate 'when a prophet speaks in the name of the Lord', to nurture a certain healthy scepticism; a posture that says, 'Okay, that's great, now let's wait and see.' (chapter 8).

Over the years I have watched Chris Westhoff's prophetic words 'come to pass' and 'come true' again and again as they did that day at the end of my 'writing' retreat. Personally she has often brought the Word of the Lord directly and accurately into my own life, and corporately into the life of the 24-7 Prayer movement. Chris is the real deal: she combines amazing supernatural insight with a reassuring natural earthiness. Her marriage is strong, her sons are wonderful. She's kind, fun, and not weird. I've often noticed her on retreats for senior leaders high in the Rocky Mountains, sitting alone on the deck early in the morning, her Bible open, a blanket around her shoulders, a steaming mug of tea in her hand, simply communing quietly with her Lord. Over many years I've witnessed the remarkable way in which Chris Westhoff's ministry truly 'speaks to people for their strengthening, encouraging and comfort' (1 Cor. 14:2), not just in 'the buckle of the Bible belt', but in the cities of post-Christian Europe, and even amongst persecuted believers in the Middle East. Some people have a prophetic gift, others have a prophetic ministry, but Chris Westhoff is recognised as one who carries the prophetic office in the worldwide 24-7 Prayer family.

Learning to discern God's voice is the single most important thing you'll ever learn to do, yet it can also be one of the most confusing and painful. Few things are more open to abuse. From manipulative parents citing Bible verses, to leaders making pronouncements about the outcome of political elections, we've all been hurt (a theme Chris explores in chapter 2). As a result, many people have walked away from faith, some have retreated altogether from prophetic ministry, and others remain wary and confused, looking for sound guidance.

In Reframing the Prophetic Chris Westhoff shares her own hard-won insights, drawn from many years of biblical reflection and underpinned by her own faithful prophetic ministry, on the front-lines of local church life around the world. This is a beautifully written and comprehensive over-view of the subject itself, alongside practical teaching for anyone seeking to grow in the prophetic gift personally, and also for leaders looking to establish a healthy prophetic culture within their congregational life. I particularly welcome the chapter on the important relationship between prophecy and creativity.

I also welcome the over-riding message of this book which relates to the healthy interface between prophetic ministry and the local church. After thirty years as a pastor, I am more convinced than ever that the apostolic and prophetic gifts are designed to work together for the health of the church. Without prophetic disruption, churches quickly becomes weak, boring and institutional. Without apostolic leadership, the prophetic quickly becomes gnostic, disembodied and weird. Which is precisely why there's always so much misunderstanding and spiritual warfare around the relationships between pastors and prophets. I would encourage all

Christian leaders therefore — whether or not you consider yourself prophetically inclined — to study this book and consider rolling out its associated course in your congregations.

I am convinced that the world does not need any more itinerant prophetic ministries, nor does it need a proliferation of lifeless, programmatic denominations, and it certainly does not need any more one-man shows (let's be honest, it is indeed almost always a man). But our world is crying out for the People of God to arise once again in our time to speak truth to power, and power to truth, for the glory of Jesus Christ.

Soli Deo gloria,

Pete Greig
Waverley Abbey, Advent 2023 founder, 24-7 Prayer International, senior pastor, Emmaus Rd, England, author *Red Moon Rising, How to Hear God, How To Pray, God on Mute,* and *Dirty Glory*

ReFraming the Prophetic

Introduction

Even with its scandalous reputation in various streams and traditions of Jesus followers, the prophetic still tugs at our imagination. Whether we find ourselves drawn toward this strange gifting or repelled away from it, we cannot deny it somehow demands our attention. Maybe it's because most of the human race has a desperate hunger to experience God's voice crashing into their slumbering lives. Whether or not we are in touch with that hunger, I'm convinced that it still rumbles somewhere deep within each and every one of us. We seem to instinctively know that His voice will reach places where mere words cannot go. But our hunger is not satiated, or even remotely appeased, through the expression of our modern-day prophetic ministry. Our longing is for something so much greater. Our longing is for union with God Himself.

The notion of God speaking to ordinary humans and then asking them to share His words with others is audacious, to say the least. It's terrifying, exhilarating, and awe-inspiring to think that God would trust us to do something so holy. It feels as though God still longs to make Himself tangible and touchable through human flesh over and over and over again. God with us, the hope of glory (Colossians 1:27). He named Himself "Emmanuel," and this tells us so much about who He is. Yet, most modern-day prophetic ministry hasn't even come close to being what Scripture reveals about this Old and New Testament gift.

This book is an exploration of the prophetic in Scripture that has been birthed out of a longing for the fullness of this calling to be seen in the earth. What we see today can't be all there is, can it? Even the most significant power encounters I've heard of and personally experienced, though they are breathtaking and transformative, leave me longing for more and filled with questions. But that's okay. I much prefer sitting in the mystery of the questions to glib, over-simplified, shallow answers. So if you're willing to lean in deeply to the questions, many of which are unanswerable but still begging to be asked, read on. This complicated, beautiful calling deserves the time it takes to paddle our way through the mysterious land of the Holy Spirit throughout Scripture. I personally believe it's crucial that we give this conversation our full attention, because we are in desperate need of healthy and mature prophetic voices in the earth today.

We haven't often seen the full expression of the New Testament prophetic gifting (if at all). The world is longing to see the Isaiahs and Ezekiels of our generation. We desperately need those who stand face to face with God and live a life that bears the mark of the uncompromising, not-so-ear-tickling, culture-dismissing, intimacy-defining prophet of God. The ones who carry the authority to turn culture, transform cities, and pull the Body of Christ into alignment with heaven. I do understand that there was a cosmic shift in the prophetic from the Old Testament to the New, and I will be discussing that later in this book. But the power of the voice of God still reverberates throughout our world today.

There's an invitation hovering in the air for anyone who is listening. It's summoning us to explore things we've taken for granted while asking the questions we've so often avoided. If we say yes to this exploration, it will inevitably require us to lean into conversations that make us uncomfortable. But the reward will be worth it. We don't know yet what we've been missing in our prophetic experience, but I believe He longs to show us.

— CHAPTER 1 —

The Holy Spirit

In 2005, David Foster Wallace shared the keynote address to the graduating class at Kenyon College. In it, he ruthlessly exposes our "unconsciousness, the default setting, the rat race, the constant gnawing sense of having had, and lost, some infinite thing." He begins with a parable:

> "There are these two young fish swimming along, and they happen to meet an older fish swimming the other way, who nods at them and says, "Morning, boys. How's the water?" And the two young fish swim on for a bit, and then eventually one of them looks over at the other and goes, "What the heck is water?"[1]

I often feel this way as I move mindlessly through my day. Revelations of the beauty of the Lord surround us. Everywhere we look, we can encounter something stunning that will declare the glory of God, if we have eyes to see it. The presence of the Holy Spirit is all around us, upon us, and within us, but we are often oblivious. We're like fish swimming in the ocean, longing for water.

I grew up in the Catholic Church and have had a life-long love affair with Jesus. As a child, I climbed trees and prayed, listening for His voice in the wind. But in 1993, I found myself in Wichita, Kansas at a Vineyard Church feeling compelled toward the Lord in new ways. I became absolutely enthralled by the Holy Spirit. My heart beat faster as I approached any kind of church gathering. I couldn't wait for our small groups on Tuesday nights, Bible studies on Thursdays, or Sunday morning gatherings. At the end of every Sunday, I counted the days until I could return.

One day, as I was driving to my Bible study, I realized that I had lived my whole life believing in Jesus but neglecting my relationship with the Holy Spirit. I realized that I had seen Him move, felt His presence, and encountered His power, but I hadn't ever talked directly to the Holy Spirit. What was I thinking?! I began right then and there.

Throughout scripture the Holy Spirit moves in a variety of ways. He gives us power to be witnesses of Christ (Acts 1:8), He empowers the fruit of love, joy, peace, patience, kindness, goodness, faithfulness and self control (Acts 5:22-23). He can appear in such a way where He sounds like a mighty rushing wind, filling the whole room with His tangible Presence (Acts 2:1-4). All experiences of the Holy Spirit are to be honored and cherished, and no one's personal experience should be held up as a standard for others. He is intimately involved in the lives of every believer. On this particular day, my experience was not common for me. As I began to talk directly to the Holy Spirit, repenting for ignoring Him, I couldn't even finish my sentence before His presence filled my car to such a degree that I couldn't drive any further. I pulled the car over to the side of the road as something that felt like waves of love poured over me. I was trembling, sobbing, and trying to talk to Him, but I couldn't form words. It felt as though He had just been waiting for me to look directly at Him, to notice and acknowledge Him as the One who was present. I stayed in this encounter with the Holy Spirit, sitting in my car on the side of the road, trembling, crying, for at least an hour. When I drove off, I knew I would never be the same.

For many years following, whenever I turned my thoughts toward the Holy Spirit, His presence would wash over me. Each time, I knew I had a choice. I could turn away, focus in another direction, change the subject, or surrender to His love. All He was asking me to do was to allow Him room in my life, my heart, and my vision. I was eager to say yes.

Soon after this encounter my husband and I started leading a small group at our church, and it was explosive. It grew so large so quickly that our senior pastors wanted to help turn it into a church plant. People were saved, bodies were healed, those experiencing homelessness were welcomed and loved, the broken were encountering the love of God, and the prophetic was bursting forth in unbridled measure. We didn't bother labeling things because we simply enjoyed dancing through our days hand in hand with the Holy Spirit, getting into some serious Kingdom mischief.

But eventually, my brokenness caught up with me. I began to receive attention for the prophetic gifting that was overflowing everywhere I turned. Before the attention, I had just enjoyed being carried along by the Holy Spirit. As the attention increased, my focus turned toward the gift itself, and things began to get funky. "Ministry" became more and more about me. I wanted to grow in my gift, and this was fine. But honestly, I became somewhat obsessed. Not to mention that I began to feel especially important!

The Lord was faithful as He patiently walked me through healing from a wounded identity, childish character, and behavior that called for repentance and restoration. My relationship with the Holy Spirit began much like many marriages do. We had a beautiful honeymoon season, but toxic pieces of my soul needed to be addressed if this relationship was to grow more deeply toward a surrendered union. These beautiful, rocky first years taught me many valuable lessons.

The gift is the Holy Spirit Himself. As we attempt to discuss any gift of the Spirit, our first conversation needs to be about developing our relationship with the Holy Spirit. Nothing happens that is of eternal value until we fix our faces upon Jesus and learn to co-create with the Holy Spirit. If prophesying is what He is doing, then let's do it well. If healing or teaching or worshiping is what He is doing, then let's do it with Him. Abiding with Him is our aim, for "in Him we live and move and have our being."*

Who is The Holy Spirit ?

We often talk about the things the Holy Spirit does, but do we truly know Him? We know He comforts, convicts, guides, sanctifies, empowers, and reveals. But what about His personality? Who is this mysterious Third Person of our trinitarian God? He was there at the beginning of Creation, hovering like a mother hen over the dark, stirring the waters ready to bring forth life. At the moment of conception, He was there with Mary, hovering over her body, about to incarnate the divine. He was there at the tomb, ready and waiting to resurrect.

His resurrection power was so potent that many others were raised from their graves at the same moment (Matthew 27:51). In the weightiest moments of Scripture, the Holy Spirit is seen resurrecting, creating, and birthing new life. He climbs into our hearts and cries "Abba! Father!" over and over again so loudly that we forget it's Him. And that is His goal: He crashes into our confusion, takes us by the hand, and pulls us into truth. The Holy Spirit mines the depths of the heart of God and implants this divine gold into our soul (1 Cor. 2:10-12). This isn't someone who seems to waste time with small talk or shallowness of heart!

He is not an atmosphere, a power surge, or an object we can learn to manipulate. He is not an electric current that turns on when we want Him to or performs at our beck and call. He is not a force that sits ready to serve our urges, nor something that happens when the room is charged with worship. He is wholly and completely Other. He is Divine in every way, the Majestic One, the Transcendent Eternal Spirit, and He is holy.

---

*   Acts 17:28 NKJV

The outrageous generosity displayed as the Father and Son pour forth the Holy Third Person amidst the darkness of sin and decay is overwhelming. Sheer, raw holiness dwelling within our tainted world, tangled up with humanity. Words fail.

His Holiness is the very thing that makes His intimate involvement in our lives so stunning. The reality that He is within us, upon us, and moving through us, as well as flowing through believers and non-believers alike in the world, is truly scandalous.

Just think of the nearness required for His gentle leading to take place. Or the communion of the Spirit that happens when He brings revelation to our minds and hearts. The affection and care revealed about the Holy Spirit being our guide and teacher has captured my imagination. The more we ponder the Spirit's involvement in our lives, the more we see how He longs to be included.

The Holy Spirit is to be seen, known, experienced, and befriended in the depths of our being. Yet, He is an utter mystery. It is easy for us to talk about the Holy Spirit as if we know and understand things about Him that we really don't know. Presumption lurks at the door of this relationship all too easily. He leads us, but most of the time doesn't tell us where. Sometimes He arrives on the scene in power, and other times He is more like a soft, nearly imperceptible breeze.

He is often the most present when we don't know He is there, and then when we think He should manifest Himself, He apparently disagrees. He doesn't seem to care about our public dignity or our planned schedules, and He certainly doesn't bow to our wishes. He truly blows where He wants, and we cannot tell where He came from or where He's going (John 3:8). I wonder if the more we try to grasp knowledge about Him, the more elusive He becomes.

It seems He will go out of His way to prove that we cannot control Him in the slightest. He won't be summoned or commanded; He will only be followed and obeyed. Yet, He desires to be a companion to us along the way. I am convinced the Holy Spirit will not allow Himself to be understood with our natural mind. Perhaps that is what Augustine of Hippo meant when he said, "If you comprehend, it is not God."[2]

He wants to be sought through the heart, through love, through encounter, and through experience because our heart can grab hold of larger realities than our brain is capable of comprehending. Our heart can engage in deeper matters, while our brain often just tries to define, pin down, control, or grasp. Any deepening relationship with the Holy Spirit must be cultivated from our hearts, befriending the mystery of who He is.

If we try to relate to the Holy Spirit with our natural, human instinct of needing to understand, feel in control, and desire to manipulate our will and our way, He won't be found. We find Him in awe and wonder, and He will only relate to us in mystery. For us to engage in this kind of relationship, we need to position our hearts in childlike surrender, gleefully captured by this beautiful, unpredictable, Holy Other.

He and I are separate individuals, and I must never forget this. In some traditions there is a temptation to ignore the Holy Spirit altogether, but it in other traditions we can use language that makes the Holy Spirit seem like He is integrated into my imagination or emotions, or some "thing" that stirs in my gut. It's easy to treat Him as an elusive "thing" floating around the atmosphere rather than the Third Person of the Trinity. This magnificent Spirit is to be worshiped, followed, adored, obeyed, and loved. He is to be honored and respected as the Holy One. He has a will and an intention to which we are beckoned to yield.

To think that the Holy Spirit is the One who breathes revelation into our heart and mind about the Father and the Son is astonishing (John 14:26). Without this Third Person, we would not know the other Two. He is ready and willing to lead us into a deeper relationship with our Trinitarian Godhead, which is good news. Because having a conversation about maturing in our prophetic calling must first and foremost begin with an honest discussion about our relationship with God, and this includes the Holy Spirit Himself. It is His gift, after all (1 Corinthians 12:1). He doesn't just give us this gift and then tell us to figure it out. He calls us to live and breathe this calling surrendered to His movement, His timing, His will, His personality, and His intention every step of the way. At the root of every prophetic word is a revelation of God, and only the Holy Spirit can truly bring this forth. It is His job as the Great Revealer.

He is the one who awakens, speaks, and transforms. Not us. He is the one who roots up, plants, delivers, corrects and instructs. Not us. The invitation from the Holy Spirit is to remain with Him, to be so wholly captivated, caught up, and enthralled with Him, lost in the wonder of who He is and what He is up to that we don't become quickly drawn to trying to understand the task at hand. The prophetic begins and ends in the context of a love affair, just as the Bible does.

The Gifts Belong to Him

Before we can talk about how we receive from the work and person of the Holy Spirit, before we talk about the gifts of the Holy Spirit or grow in the prophetic, we must first and always orient our focus on the Person of the Holy Spirit. As we begin to discuss the gifts of the Holy Spirit, one of our ground rules is that the gifts do not belong to us.

I remember back in the early 2000s when the Swine Flu was in full swing. It was a frightening time as we heard of the death toll rising from this horrible sickness every day. I was in the middle of a challenging ministry trip in Serbia. My heart was homesick, sleep was elusive, my team was off-kilter, and there were many other challenges. One night as I climbed into bed, I opened my phone and saw that my husband had texted. Sam, our youngest son, had the Swine Flu. I curled up in a ball and sobbed like a baby. I felt so very far away (as I was!) and powerless to do anything at all. As I lay there for hours and hours, all I could do was cry out to the Lord. I expressed my fear and anxiety over being so far away and allowed my overwhelming sadness to flow freely before the Lord. I felt like a toddler who just needed to emote until there was nothing left to say and no more tears to be found.

At the end of my wave of emotion, I gently gave Sam over to the Lord. In my imagination, I picked up my son and put him in God's hands. Then I let go. I felt the Lord speak to me and say, "Sam is MY son. I have been holding him all along." As this gentle reminder washed over my soul, I said, "Yes, of course You have."

I'm sure many other parents reading this could tell similar stories. We need to be regularly reminded of who is really in charge and that God the Father loves our children more than we ever could. They are a gift given to us, yet they belong fully and entirely to God. We are invited daily to carefully take part in their lives, but we should never forget that they belong to the Lord first. (Sam recovered nicely, by the way).

If this is true of our children, how much more is it true of spiritual gifts to which we have even less claim and that are of less eternal importance than the children in our care? They are gifts given by the Holy Spirit, but they are not things we can claim with sole ownership. I see this prophetic gifting in my life as one of those things that simply doesn't belong to me. It originates in the heart of God and is given, moved, inspired, empowered, initiated, birthed, and carried out by the Holy Spirit. And He is wholly and completely Other, meaning He is a separate and distinct God/person. He is other than us, other than the world, other than humanity, and an "other" in the Trinity.

In the Bible, we read about this guy named Simon, a sorcerer (Acts 8). He was a respected and sought-after person in the community and known for his spiritual powers. He encountered the disciples and experienced a legitimate salvation moment in which he believed in the Lord Jesus. But then he witnessed how God poured out the Spirit through the apostles' hands and he wanted this power! Of course he did. Just think of his history. Using supernatural power for his personal benefit is all he knew. So he offered them money and said,

"Give me also this ability so that everyone on whom I lay my hands may receive the Holy Spirit." Peter answered: "May your money perish with you, because you thought you could buy the gift of God with money! You have no part or share in this ministry, because your heart is not right before God'"*.

Can you hear Peter's shock? Can you hear his heart jolt backward as this man objectifies the One he loves? Can you see the two worlds clashing? Even though Simon had a saving knowledge of Jesus Christ, his mind was not renewed. His thought process was still functioning through his old constructs, value systems, and understanding. His whole life had taught him to use the spiritual realm to accomplish his own purposes. He was well-trained within a world that permitted him to objectify spiritual power for his benefit, giving him a feeling of significance. Within this worldly point of view, supernatural power was lusted after because it offered a sense of importance. This is all he knew.

And this is all many of us know as we enter into this dynamic Kingdom. The paradigm of objectifying that which offers worldly rewards is natural human behavior. It's our immature soul trying to work out our identity, tripping over our self-centered approach to love. If we're honest with ourselves, we have all struggled with this temptation. Spiritual gifts make us feel important.

This story is powerful because it shows the stark contrast between Simon's paradigm and Peter's. We see the constructs of the world coming

---

*   Acts 8:18-20 NIV

into sharp conflict with the value system of the Kingdom. Peter is standing before Simon with a heart that has been captured and a mind that has been drenched in a loving, cherished, humble relationship with the Third Person of the Trinity. Simon's offer to purchase the One Peter loves is deeply wounding to his soul. It is a violation of the purity of the Holy Spirit, who was Peter's most cherished companion.

Our greatest gift of all is the Holy Spirit dwelling within us as a temple not made with hands (Acts 7:48). This revelation should drop us to our knees, plain and simple. Once we understand who He is, we will take His hand regardless of where He leads us. But often, probably more than we care to admit, He will need to remind us that the gifts belong to Him because, like Simon, we try to grasp His power for our own purposes.

In the early 2000s, there was a surge of people being raised from the dead throughout Mozambique. We heard story after story of people praying for the dead and seeing them awaken. Friends of ours traveled to Mozambique to witness this for themselves and wanted to learn everything they could from what the Lord was doing. They told us the story of being ushered into a grass hut arranged like a conference room. There was a large folding table and several chairs on a dirt floor. As my friends waited in this room, the ministry leader brought in several of the local pastors and had them sit around the table.

The leader began to make introductions, casually saying each of their names and telling our friends how many people each one had raised from the dead. "This is so-and-so, and they've raised 14 people from the dead. This is so-and-so, and they've raised 26 people from the dead" and so on. Within minutes, the room exploded into utter chaos as each and every one of these indigenous leaders threw themselves under the table, burying their faces into the dirt, throwing the earth over their heads, and screaming, "No!! It wasn't us!! We can't take any of the glory! It wasn't us! It was the Lord alone!!!" And they wouldn't get up to show their faces again until my friends had left the room. They remained under the table weeping, with their faces in the dirt, until the Americans had left the room.

In some Charismatic or Pentecostal traditions today, we think nothing of taking a video of ourselves praying for someone or telling stories of how the Holy Spirit moved through us in power and posting it on Facebook. It makes me wonder if there is part of our culture that is dangerously like Simon the Sorcerer in how we relate to the Holy Spirit. My prayer today is that we will have eyes to see and ears to hear as Peter did and that we will treat this beautiful Third Person of the Trinity as the most precious, holy, awe-inspiring gift of our lives.

If someone asked me to tell them about my marriage and I began to describe it as this realm that I could engage with, learn to maneuver in, have fun experiences with, etc., it would feel strange, wouldn't it? Even though it wouldn't be totally inaccurate, it would be an odd, offensive way to talk about something so sacred. And it wouldn't come close to offering a healthy paradigm on marriage. Marriage is about a love affair between two people who become one, forever joined in covenant, each laying their lives down for the other. It sometimes feels too deep to try to put into words. I feel the same way about the Holy Spirit. To talk about the Spirit as a realm, a power we can steward, or some cool thing we can learn to experience feels like a violation of the depth of this love story.

When we are face to face with Christ at the end of the age, I can guarantee you that the prophetic, or powerful encounters, signs and wonders, or big important callings won't be on our minds. We will be so blissfully caught up in love with the King that our spiritual gifts, callings, and missions will be nothing but a faint memory. So as we engage in this scriptural conversation about the prophetic, please promise me that you will continually remind yourself that this is about the Holy Spirit and His mission on the earth. This is about co-laboring in love with a vision toward an eternal dream. His mission and purpose are the point. Not the prophetic. The prophetic is just one small way the Holy Spirit moves through us doing what He does best: bringing glory to the person of Jesus Christ.

From beginning to end, the whole God-story is about the Kingdom of God flourishing and expanding throughout the earth. Like gnats that buzz around our heads, this life has many distractions that take too much of our attention. If a house builder became obsessed with his hammer and began to believe that the hammer was the point, he would cease to be a good builder. We can easily find ourselves preoccupied with the things of the Spirit rather than the Holy Spirit Himself and miss the sacred story unfolding right under our nose.

Seeing Him for Who He Is

John tells of the intimate dinner that Jesus and His disciples had that is commonly known as the Last Supper. This is a critical moment in their journey. Judas has just left with betrayal in his heart, and Jesus begins sharing some of His final words with His disciples (John 14–18). These words will carry the disciples through the next few traumatic days. Jesus says,

"I will ask the Father, and He will give you another Helper, so that He may be with you forever; the Helper is the Spirit of truth, whom the world cannot receive, because it does not see Him or know Him; but you know Him because He remains with you and will be in you."*

Can you hear it? Jesus is encouraging and comforting His disciples with the promise of the indwelt Holy Spirit. He knows what is about to happen. He is looking into the future and preparing them for His departure. It is a sobering moment. These disciples must have been confused and frightened. But oh, how excited Jesus is about the One who is to come!

---

* John 14:16–17

If His followers only knew the treasure they were about to receive! The Holy Spirit, who is the most profound gift of all, will be given by God in a new way to dwell within His followers. "These things I have spoken to you while remaining with you. But the Helper, the Holy Spirit whom the Father will send in My name, He will teach you all things, and remind you of all that I said to you."*

Everything that these disciples have experienced in their living and breathing relationship with Jesus they will soon share with the Holy Spirit. He will speak the truth. He will help. He will remind them of everything Jesus told them. Beautiful! But then Jesus drops this bomb: "But you know Him because He remains with you and will be in you."† Wait, WHAT? The Holy Spirit has been here the whole time?!

The disciples knew of the Holy Spirit already, of course. They had the Torah, and they knew the stories of the One who had hovered over the waters during Creation. They knew He had empowered David, made Samson strong, and filled the mouths of the prophets. They knew of the Spirit of God but did not understand Him in trinitarian terms. They referred to the Holy Spirit as Yahweh in action. But at this moment, Jesus is explaining to them that they know Him. Jesus is directly telling them, "You do know Him!"

It makes me think that these men had been experiencing the Holy Spirit all this time but had not yet understood that they were going to be personally invited into an active relationship with Him. It's as if a family member had been staying in their home this whole time but they hadn't known him face to face. Jesus made the introduction. He was making sure they actually saw this family member who had been hovering around them, and He informed them that their relationship was about to take on a whole new meaning. The Holy Spirit was going to dwell within them.

---

* John 14:25-26
† John 14:17

These poor fishermen, tax collectors, and uneducated peasants were going to receive the indwelling of the Holy Spirit? It is shocking for sure. Up until this time, only the prophets, kings, and chosen ones had received the Holy Spirit. I can only imagine how these very normal humans felt as they heard these words.

I can picture Jesus speaking these words to us personally. "You know Him. He's been living in your house for many years now." Maybe you haven't taken the time to look Him in the face and call Him by name. He's dwelling within you, and He's moving through you. He's comforting you, teaching you, leading you into truth, and reminding you of everything Jesus has spoken. "You have received a Spirit of adoption as sons and daughters by which we cry out, 'Abba! Father!'"* He reminds you that you are, in fact, a child of God. This Holy Spirit is the source of God's love being poured into your hearts (Romans 5:5). He is the One you need.

---

*   Romans 8:15

— CHAPTER 2 —

Something Is Wrong

I think it's safe to say that the prophetic gift we see, or don't see, functioning today isn't the fullness of what it is called to be. In some circles it has taken on a form that no longer looks anything like what we see in Scripture, and in other circles (possibly as a reaction to the former) they have shut it down altogether. I think most would agree that we are not experiencing the scriptural call of the prophetic in its fullness. We know there's more. There must be more.

Yes, the individual prophetic ministry that we are familiar with in many circles, in which we speak into someone's identity, build them up in encouragement, and edify their soul with the loving words of the Lord is beautiful. I love this, and I think we should do this as often as possible. Simply put, He has better words than we do; words of love, truth, and beauty. Inviting Him into these spaces of encouragement is very important. Learning to hear His voice is crucial.

Yet, I have to admit that some of the ways I have seen the prophetic function over the years has caused my heart to ache. There have been times that I have left church meetings with a pit in my stomach, knowing that something wasn't quite right but being unsure exactly what it was. I felt as if we were teaching people how to put up their antennas to sense and feel the realm of the Spirit, which can be useful for good discernment. But this is not the same as truly teaching people to hear the voice of God.

Are we teaching people the difference between being spiritually sensitive and rightly hearing the voice of God? It seems that many people just learn to put their spiritual antennas up and label everything as God's voice. This in and of itself is a problem that often bites us in the proverbial behind. But I knew it was more than that. It has felt as if something in the root system was off. There are the obvious issues of pride, character, etc., but I have been sensing something deeper to be addressed. For a long time I had trouble seeing through the fog of confusion to grab hold of the real problem.

Many of us tried our best to teach people how to set the right boundaries around the prophetic, probably hoping that this would at least help stem the damage. Many leaders within prophetic communities would cling to Scripture passages that highlighted encouragement and exhorted prophetic people to be moved by love and to pursue love. This was all good advice. Still, I had an unscratchable itch somewhere in the back of my head that something was deeply wrong. Is it possible that some things have been taught so often by so many that they've become normative and presumed biblical? Is it possible that some of our understanding of the prophetic has evolved into something that no longer resembles what we see on the pages of Scripture?

For me this was a frightening question. There is something deeply disorienting about questioning things that you have believed for many years. It is like the earth trembling beneath your feet and throwing off your equilibrium to such a degree that you don't know what you can grab hold of to stabilize yourself. But the questions that had been trying to find their voice for several years were forcing themselves to the surface, and I didn't seem to have a choice.

Then 2020 happened. In the midst of a global pandemic, the United States was shrouded in clouds of racial pain, political polarization, conspiracy theories, and divisive eruptions on every level. If this wasn't enough, some of the most beloved charismatic prophetic voices seemed to be adding fuel to the fire through their prophecies. My phone was ringing off the hook from pastors, prophets, and leaders from multiple countries trying to make sense of it all.

Then, when their prophecies didn't come true, several of them repented publicly. This was humble and honorable, but it brought even more questions to the surface. Every time my phone rang, I dreaded the inevitable conversation that was going to unfold. I didn't have any easy answers for anyone. I felt as if we were experiencing the fruit of a certain tree, and it wouldn't benefit anyone just to talk about the fruit. We needed to dig into the roots and take another look at the whole tree.

This wasn't about politics. This wasn't about this prophet's words compared to that prophet's words, if they were right or wrong, or if maybe they were partly right but missed this piece or that piece. There was a much bigger conversation that needed to happen, and we were now forced to dig this tree up and see what it was made of.

As I dove headlong into a fresh round of studies, talking with trusted theologians and asking the bold, difficult questions to the right people, I quickly realized that I could find myself in the quicksand of analysis if I continued to try to dissect what was wrong. It felt like trying to catch 50 marbles as they rolled on a plate. It was frustrating, to say the least. As I was holding all of this in prayer, I felt the Lord gently draw my attention toward counterfeit currency. I had heard that the experts in spotting the counterfeit were not trained by studying the imitations but by examining the real currency. They studied until they became so intimate with the authentic, so deeply familiar with the true currency that anything other would stick out like a sore thumb. The more they knew the real, the easier it was to spot the false.

So that is what I decided to do. I was going to gaze at the prophets of old, not just study them from a distance. I was going to watch them closely, meditate upon their lives, and try to sense who they were and what moved them. I needed to deeply contemplate Isaiah, Ezekiel, David and Amos, Huldah, Miriam, Deborah, John the Baptist, Ananias, Mary, Elizabeth, Peter, and Paul. I wanted to imagine their humanity, ponder their emotions, and consider their lives.

As I did this, I felt as if I was watching the Spirit of Prophecy as the main character in this epic story. He emerged through various people, but the same Spirit was clearly visible. The questions began to bubble up within me. What is He actually doing? What is He wanting to accomplish through these prophetic voices? Once I could recognize this Spirit of Prophecy, I found myself caught up in observing the passion, mission, and purpose of the prophetic. I felt as if I was truly seeing the true prophetic in motion for the first time. It was both exhilarating and devastating.

I found myself trying to picture the apostle Paul sitting in our prophetic conferences. The great apostle who wrote from behind prison doors that he had lost everything and didn't care one bit because he had been captured by the beauty of Jesus; the apostle Paul who loved the Lord so desperately that he could only bring himself to preach one thing: Christ and Him crucified; the apostle Paul who had discovered the treasure in the field, and it had ruined his taste for anything else.

I would try to picture Paul sitting next to me as some prophet was on stage wowing the crowd with his knowledge of a dead loved one, telling us to call down money from heaven, or calling out names, dates or addresses of people in the crowd as they gasped and cheered. I would imagine Isaiah, Ezekiel, or John the Beloved sitting in the room during one of my prophetic workshops, and I just wanted to lay down on the floor and groan in grief and cry out in repentance for weeks. In fact, that is exactly what I did.

As we read the stories of the New Testament, we see the prophetic woven throughout almost every page. We see the prophetic gift moving when Ananias was told by the Lord to seek out the violent persecutor named Saul and to pray for his blind eyes to be opened, thus, igniting and propelling one of the most influential men in human history into his calling (Acts 9:10-19).

We read in wonder about Peter on the rooftop caught up in a prophetic vision that he didn't understand (Acts 10:9-16), and somewhat simultaneously, Cornelius had a prophetic encounter and sent men to fetch Peter. Through this series of prophetic visions, the Gospel broke through the barriers of division, and the Gentiles were ushered into the Body of Christ.

We see the prophetic intervene as the Macedonian man appeared before Paul and catapulted the Gospel into Europe (Acts 16:8-10). We see the prophetic assuring the men who were on the boat with Paul that they would survive, because God intended Paul to stand before Caesar and take the Gospel to Rome (Acts 27:21-25).

Just as Ananias opened the eyes of Paul, we are able to see that the prophetic is the vision that brings forth the revelation upon which the apostolic builds. We see the warnings, the corrections, the instructions, and the directions. The prophetic paved the way for the Gospel over and over again. The prophets in the Bible were not fortune tellers. Their purpose was not predicting the future, and they certainly didn't put on conferences where their entire focus was encouraging individuals with personal words.

One of the primary idols of our Western culture is comfort.Everything we do is motivated by comfort. Our value systems are designed around comfort, and many of our church services are created for comfort. I know it sounds harsh, but every culture on the planet has their idols, and idols create filters through which we perceive the world around us. These filters also influence how we read our Bibles. Is it possible that our Western understanding of the prophetic has been influenced by our cultural idol of comfort? Not a far-fetched idea at all.

By the end of this book, I believe you'll see clearly that the call of the New Testament prophetic is to stand rooted firmly with their eyes fixed on the person of Jesus. Prophets are to be anchored in the eternal purposes of Christ, to proclaim and declare the words and intentions of God, and to pull the Church into alignment with the will of heaven, keeping us rightly anchored on our eternal path. This is what we see in Scripture. In fact, theologians agree that in the Bible we see that the purpose of the prophetic is to call the people of God into alignment with the covenant. We'll speak more about this later.

I am not saying that all of the prophetic ministry that we see today is bad or wrong. There are some beautiful things the Lord has done through the prophetic in our day. Not everything is off base, and not everything we have known or understood is unbiblical. Truly, I have seen the prophetic flowing in ways that are redemptive and holy. We don't need to throw out the proverbial baby with the bath water, but we do need to proceed bravely into this discussion and be willing to take a closer look at the bath water.

I am aware that it is never comfortable for us when our foundations begin to shake. It is incredibly vulnerable to ask the hard questions, especially concerning things that we hold dear. Our security may feel threatened as we look at the Bible and then look at some of the modern-day uses of this gift. Yet we simply must. It is too easy for us to measure truth according to an enculturated paradigm. I believe God is inviting us into a prophetic reformation. And it includes all of us...not just the prophetic ones. It includes pastors, leaders, and the whole Body of Christ. It is an invitation to reframe our paradigm into a biblical understanding of this gift.

Can we discern when a prophecy is upheld by toxic theology? Have we trained our heart and spirit, as well as the hearts and spirits of those in our care, how to spot false prophecies? Can we rightly separate the voice of the Holy Spirit from the voice of another? Can we hear His voice above the noise or discern the will of God above our culture? Are we swallowing anything that the famous prophets speak without stopping to discern? Are we overly impressed with charisma?

Are we all fluent in the true, full Gospel, anchored deeply enough to feel a warning in the pit of our stomach when something leads us in a different direction? We need the prophetic gifting now more than ever. Is it possible that the enemy has worked diligently to keep this gift maligned, misdirected, and minimized in order to disempower its full purpose?

But God.

God will have His way.

This is our moment. This is an invitation to go deeper into Scripture, into His voice, into this life we live by the Holy Spirit, and into understanding what it means to be led by the Holy Spirit. We are invited to depend on Him for our every move. I believe with all of my heart that the Lord is beckoning us to learn what the true prophetic is called to do, to be, and to represent. We are being called to learn the voice, the movement, the mission, and the ways of the Holy Spirit so intimately that there will be no room for the counterfeit to flourish.

Let's dive into Scripture and cultivate a biblical imagination together. This is our invitation to reclaim this sacred gift and fight for its true purpose.

— CHAPTER 3 —

Old Testament Prophets

The prophetic is an ancient gift. Its lineage stretches back to Abel (Luke 11:50-51), but some have referred to Adam as the first prophet. In order to understand this powerful gift that is still in our midst, I believe it is essential that we take time to look at the Old Testament prophets and learn from these mighty, awe-inspiring, and terrifying individuals. It is also vital that we discuss how this gift changed in the transition from the Old to the New Testament.

I believe that a cosmic shift of the prophetic happened after the death and resurrection of Christ that was consummated at Pentecost. Many theologians point both to Jesus and John the Baptist as having similar characteristics of the Old Testament prophets. They brought declarations from God to the people of Israel, most often in public settings, that were often correcting sin, addressing false understanding, teaching about the Kingdom, and warning of judgment to come. After Pentecost, though, we see a massive shift. The prophetic is seen to continually and supernaturally pave the way for the revelation of the Kingdom of God.

One of the major reasons the prophetic appeared to be so different in the New Testament is the role of the Holy Spirit. Of course, there is much activity of the Holy Spirit throughout the Old Testament. We see Him upon and within prophets, kings, and priests. He performs many signs and wonders, fills Solomon's temple, and empowers people to prophesy, heal, build, and deliver nations. Yet, at Pentecost, the Spirit was poured out in a new way on all flesh (Acts 2).

In the Old Testament, we see individuals who are anointed with power for certain tasks. Now we see the whole Church filled with the power and presence of God to declare the truth of Jesus Christ and proclaim God's mighty deeds. The sons and daughters are now the temple of God on the earth, and they are all empowered to hear God's voice and to move in the gifts of the Spirit. This shifts the dynamic entirely. For one thing, we see the prophetic functioning with dramatically different levels of authority. In the Old Testament, the Israelites were commanded to listen to the prophets and do what they said, period. In the New Testament, prophets are commanded to submit to the community to test and weigh their messages.

In the Old Testament, the prophets led nations into battle and guided the hearts of kings. In the New Testament, the Church is led by elders and deacons, and the foundations are laid by the apostles, prophets, evangelists, pastors, and teachers working together (Ephesians 4:11). In the Old Testament, prophets were stoned for being wrong. In the New Testament, we are to test prophetic utterances and hold fast only to that which is good. Many of the Old Testament prophets lived alone in the desert and were separated from society. In the New Testament, most prophetic moments are in the context of relationship—the prophets moved in and among the community of believers. Ephesians 4 also reveals that the prophets are part of a bigger picture, one slice of a pie, one part of a team that has a common goal. This is dramatically different from the role of the prophets in the Old Testament.

What Didn't Change

The bigger question might be, What is the same? Has this gift shifted so dramatically from the Old Testament to the New Testament that it no longer bears any resemblance? Is this even the same gift? The majority of the Old Testament prophets spoke direction, correction, and warning to the nation of Israel. Every now and then we see them speaking to other nations, such as Moses to Pharaoh about Egypt. It is only in a couple of places that we see a prophet directly speaking a word from the Lord to an individual, as in the story of Nathan and David (2 Samuel 12). Except for these rare moments, it is safe to say that the primary focus of the Old Testament prophets was the alignment of Israel to the covenant, which was given as a framework in which Israel was to be in relationship with God.

In the New Testament, post-Pentecost, we see many more individual moments of prophecy, such as Ananias to Paul (Acts 9:10-19), Peter and Cornelius (Acts 10), and Agabus to Paul (Acts 11:27-29). Many of these prophetic moments seem to be paving the way for the unfolding of the Great Commission (Matthew 28:16-20).

Did this give the prophetic a new purpose? I don't think so. If the purpose and call of the prophets in the Old Testament was to speak alignment to the covenant, then I believe the primary change was the covenant itself. As we observe the prophetic through Scripture in the coming chapters, we will undoubtedly discover that the purpose and call of the prophetic remains, from start to finish, to communicate the inspired declaration of God, calling the sons and daughters of the Kingdom into alignment with the will of God and the eternal purposes of Christ.

So let's start our observation in the most logical place, the Old Testament prophets. I say this a bit in jest because these terrifying men and women aren't usually the first place our modern-day mindsets take us when we think about the prophetic. This, I believe, is part of the problem. In many Christian circles, we have practically divorced the calling of the Old Testament prophets from the prophetic in the 21st century.

On one level, this is understandable. They're not the most comfortable people to observe! These men and women have confronted us, frightened us, called us higher, and stunned us into silence. The way they walked the earth seemed other-worldly, so it is easiest to put them in a box and tuck them away somewhere. But I believe that we simply can't discuss the prophetic gift without honoring these mysterious ones who blazed the trail.

We understand that New Testament prophetic ministry is different from the calling of these mighty men and women, but we must not use this as an excuse to discount their lives. They are not irrelevant. These exceptional human beings are our mentors, teachers, heroes, and role models. Their words still resound in our ears as layers of meaning continue to unfold thousands of years after they were penned. They continue to call us into an eternal reality that is even more expansive than they probably realized, stoking the fire of passion and the awe of God in our souls.

We learn just as much from who they were as human beings as we do from their prophetic utterances. These prophets may seem like supernatural giants in our imagination, but they were just as human as you and I. Their emotions were raw, their hearts were fragile, their minds were often tortured, and they walked this earth with the same skin and bones that hold you and me together today.

The prophet is a person, not a microphone. He is endowed with a mission, with the power of a word not his own that accounts for his greatness…but also with a temperament, concern, character, and individuality.[3] [sic][4]

They were human, so we don't have the luxury of putting them in a separate box, allowing us to detach from their struggles. When we allow ourselves to identify with the Old Testament prophets as fellow sojourners on our human path, we open our hearts to be confronted by their choices, their passions, and most of all, their surrendered abandon to the eternal mission of Yahweh.

The voice of God reverberated in and through human beings from the very beginning. Many people today discuss the prophetic in very casual ways. But when we take a good look at Isaiah, Ezekiel, Jeremiah, Amos, etc. We are forced to reckon with the tremble. God, Yahweh, the Holy One, the Majestic Other, put His voice within fallen human flesh. He apprehended these men and women and chose them as His messengers, yet He did not transform them into perfect humans beforehand. He left them utterly and completely human, with their fears, tempers, and judgments intact. He partnered with these broken and frail humans, even knowing the mess they could make.

Discussing how to contemplate the prophets, Abraham Heschel writes:

> We must think as if we were inside their minds. For them to be alive and present to us, we must think, not about, but in the prophets, with their concern and their heart. Their existence involves us. Unless their concern strikes us, pains us, or exalts us, we do not sense it. Such involvement requires accord, receptivity, hearing, sheer surrender to their impact.[5]

As we read the Old Testament prophetic books, we first need to think about the person who was speaking. These people were not just passing along two-dimensional words as if they were texting information they heard hovering in the atmosphere. They felt it was essential to communicate their emotions, experiences, anguish, and ecstasy. Their whole story mattered.

I love that Jeremiah shared his fear and doubt in chapter one of his book. He invited us into his holy encounter, sharing his emotional process along the way. He didn't need to do that! What made him share so deeply? What made him write such things as, "My anguish, my anguish! I writhe in pain! Oh, the walls of my heart! My heart is beating wildly; I cannot keep silent; for I hear the sound of the trumpet, the alarm of war."* Why didn't he make sure he only shared what God was speaking? That is what we are usually told to do. Yet Jeremiah takes time to pen it all, forever documenting his very personal, intimate struggle. And what a gift he has given us all.

Don't get me wrong—I don't think it is bad for us to work on sorting through where God's voice ends and our soul begins. I actually believe it is an important thing to work on. Yet Jeremiah included his anguish and chose to vulnerably express the depth of his emotional struggle in response to the visions he was seeing. By including these words, he exposes the level of connection that he has with it all—the passion and intention of God, the story of Israel, the impact his words had on his people, and the prophetic words themselves. Heschel writes:

> The prophet's theme is, first of all, the very life of a whole people, and his identification lasts more than a moment. He is one not only with what he says; he is involved with his people in what his words foreshadow. This is the secret of the prophets' style: his life and soul are at stake in what he says and in what is going to happen to what he says. It is an involvement that echoes on.[6]

To think that we will not feel what we see or hear from the Lord is ludicrous. In fact, it would signal a dangerous level of emotional disconnection. We feel. We are supposed to feel. It makes us human, and our humanity is a vital part of this prophetic story. Jeremiah's humanity and our humanity is not to be set aside as something uninvolved and disconnected. It makes me wonder if the humanity expressed in this prophet's documentation could be seen as a signpost that points toward the embodiment of the Word in the incarnation of Christ. The Old Testament

---

*   Jeremiah 4:19 ESV

prophets seem to understand that their humanity was an essential part of their prophetic expression. They didn't have a disembodied spirituality that could somehow discuss spiritual growth as a separate pathway to fulfillment. They were whole people who were encountering a whole story. Every word they spoke had an impact on them in ways we have a hard time grasping in our siloed culture.

> To the prophets, God was overwhelmingly real and shatter-
> ingly present. They never spoke of Him from a distance. They lived
> as witnesses, struck by the words of God, rather than as explorers
> engaged in an effort to ascertain the nature of God.[7]

This is wholeheartedness on display, and it exposes so many of our modern mindsets. With those mindsets, we can tend to see the spiritual realm as a land to conquer rather than a living, breathing people who are utterly given over—spirit, soul, and body—to the heart and passion of Yahweh. The prophet's agony preaches a whole sermon, directly poking at our arrogant detachment.

The conflict of the prophet that is witnessed in his writing as he feels the fire of God, the love of his own people, and the sin that separates the two teaches us more than we can usually bear. We can almost feel the tearing that is happening within them. This is why the humanity of the prophets matters. This is why their agony needs to be heard and why their struggle needs to be honored.

> The prophet is not a mouthpiece, but a person; not an instrument, but a partner,
> an associate of God. Emotional detachment would be understandable only if there
> were a command which required the suppression of emotion, forbidding one to

serve God "with all your heart, with all your soul, with all your might." God, we are told, asks not only for "works," for action, but above all for love, awe, and fear.[8]

As I read Jeremiah's authentic lament, I am reminded that he is in the same boat in which I often find myself. It strangely, yet beautifully, connects me with Jeremiah, even though our lives are separated by over 2600 years and radically different worlds. Jeremiah and I are fellow pilgrims, sojourners who are hearing the voice of God and encountering the pain of the world together. We are unified in our humanity. Here is this Old Testament prophet who some have exalted to a high and holy place, and he chooses to share his humanity with us. He invites us into his personal experience and reminds us that we are all in this together. We are human. And humans matter to the Lord.

What drove these men and women? What pulled them, moved them, and compelled them in their vision? What propelled them forward in their intensely difficult lives? Their actions were often shocking. Isaiah, for example, walked around naked for three years (Isaiah 20:1-4). Ezekiel lay on his side for endless days and nights (Ezekiel 4:4). To think of very human men and women intentionally walking through such extreme sacrificial and painful demonstrations should cause us to stop and ask deeper questions. Oversimplified, cheap answers just won't cut it.

Instead of showing us a way through the elegant mansions of the mind, the prophets take us to the slums. The world is a proud place, full of beauty, but the prophets are scandalized, and rave as if the whole world were a slum.[9]

They seemed to be standing in the courts of heaven with eyes that were seeing a different reality, ears that were tuned to a different dimension, and hearts that were pounding with a different purpose from the rest of us. It is as if they physically felt every crack that could bring Israel into disharmony with God, and it was unbearable to them.

> The things that horrified the prophets are even now daily occurrences all over the world. There is no society to which Amos' words would not apply.[10]

> "They hate him who reproves in the gate,
>
> And they abhor him who speaks with integrity.
>
> Therefore because you impose heavy rent on the poor
>
> And exact a tribute of grain from them,
>
> Though you have built houses of well-hewn stone,
>
> Yet you will not live in them;
>
> You have planted pleasant vineyards, yet you will not drink their wine.
>
> For I know your transgressions are many and your sins are great,
>
> You who distress the righteous and accept bribes
>
> And turn aside the poor in the gate.
>
> Therefore at such a time the prudent person keeps silent, for it is an evil time.
>
> Seek good and not evil, that you may live;
>
> And thus may the LORD God of hosts be with you,
>
> Just as you have said!
>
> Hate evil, love good
>
> And establish justice in the gate!"*

Indeed, the sort of crimes and even the amount of delinquency that fill the prophets of Israel with dismay do not go beyond that which we regard as normal, as typical ingredients of social dynamics. To us a single act of injustice—cheating in business, exploitation of the poor—is slight; to the prophets, a disaster. To us injustice is injurious to the welfare of the people;

---

*   Amos 5:10-15

to the prophets it is a death blow to existence: to us, an episode; to them, a catastrophe, a threat to the world.

> They speak and act as if the sky were about to collapse
> because Israel has become unfaithful to God.*

Herein lies their single-mindedness. Here is the reality that brings me to tears. Their connection to the heart of God and His passion for the human race keeps these prophets living in the in-between. They lived between the view of true glory and the shattering inability of Israel to keep the covenant, while holding in their bones the longing of God for His people. This is the space in which prophetic ones must learn to dwell, even today. This calling will invite us to simultaneously keep our hearts captivated with the longing of God and torn in two by the jolting contrast of what the world has become—never turning away from the white-hot love of the Father over it all.

This is the in-between, where the Old Testament prophets stood, and somehow, this empowered them to see with different eyes. They were convinced that the world's reality was contingent upon compatibility with God, so that became their only point of reference for all of life.

> The words the prophet utters are not offered as souvenirs. His speech to the
> people is not a reminiscence, a report, a hearsay. The prophet not only conveys;
> he reveals. He almost does unto others what God does unto him. In speaking,
> the prophet reveals God. This is the marvel of a prophet's work: in his words,
> the invisible God becomes audible. He does not prove or argue. The thought

---

* Ibid.

he has to convey is more than language can contain. Divine power bursts in their words. The authority of the prophet is in the Presence his words reveal.[11]

The Old Testament prophets were often referred to as covenant lawyers because their entire purpose and mission was to call Israel back to the Torah. I believe the purpose of the prophetic today remains as an echo of it's Old Testament purpose. Though it has gone through a cosmic shift, the prophetic is still supposed to be speaking forth the words of the Lord that align the Body of Christ with the new covenant - the covenant of Christ Jesus. Hence the reason why the testimony of Jesus is the spirit of prophecy (Revelation 19:10). He is the covenant.

CHAPTER 4

Jesus

Jesus should be the beginning and the end of every teaching on the prophetic. We will all read this statement and nod our heads in agreement, but what does it mean? I have gone to many prophetic conferences and read multiple books on the subject of prophecy, and I have listened to dozens and dozens of teachings on the prophetic. I can tell you with confidence that Jesus is rarely mentioned. Isn't that odd? In some circles, there is more talk of angels, portals, or traveling to heaven than of Jesus. Those teachers most likely love Jesus and follow Him with their whole hearts. Yet, for some reason, it seems frighteningly easy to set Jesus aside when the prophetic is discussed.

In our Hollywood-infused Christian culture, we often define a "great call from God" as one that is synonymous with power and fame, being a world changer, or having influence with presidents and kings. This is simply not the way of Jesus. Our cultural value of social power can lead us by the nose if we're not careful. Many of the "words of the Lord" that prophetic people call out from the front are words that build up the ego, stroke someone's idea of importance, or promise great wealth and prestige. Is it possible that our cultural idols of power and influence have affected our prophetic voices? Absolutely.

When the prophetic empowers the wrong things, such as our high value for comfort, celebrity status, or false identities, we can find ourselves engaging with something other than the Holy Spirit. We are all susceptible to deception, and we need to grow in our awareness of what kind of spirit or human will is at play. The more we can learn to discern the fighting currents of our culture, the better. None of us are immune to being influenced by social pressure. The power of a room that is filled with human desires, needs, and wants can be seductive and can mimic the leading of the Holy Spirit.

Our pursuit is Jesus, the King of the universe, the Majestic One, a humble, beautiful servant who washes His disciples' feet. As we follow the true Jesus closely, we will hopefully grow in our ability to recognize when something other than Him is taking center stage.

It's not just the spiritual world that is challenging to navigate. Humans are complex, and we're the ones the Lord is using to communicate His words. At any given point, there are many conflicting forces swirling around inside of us, often jumbled up together. We all have a variety of motives, reactions, and judgments inside of us. We can respond to love, compassion, desire, fear, control, longing, God's voice, the voice of pain, and our will that wants to push its own agenda. We are human, and our humanity is beautiful—but not simple. Finding the voice of the Lord through the rubble and debris of our interior noise can be challenging.

We will discuss the layers of our soul and its effect on the prophetic in a future chapter, but it's important to mention it here as a reminder of this beautiful, messy life we live that is filled with both glory and tragedy. This is why, as we talk about the times the prophetic has gone off course, it is vital that we remain in an attitude of mercy and compassion. It matters. It matters that we keep anchored in Christ. It matters that we acknowledge when things are off. We must learn to see the true path of maturity.

Judgment and accusation are never okay. Yet it is important that we speak openly and honestly about the things that don't seem right and learn to handle them with humility, honor, and truth. We need discernment in the Body of Christ more than ever.

"And it is my prayer that your love may abound more and more, with knowledge and all discernment, so that you may approve what is excellent, and so be pure and blameless for the day of Christ, filled with the fruit of righteousness that comes through Jesus Christ, to the glory and praise of God.".*

Recently I was with our 24-7 Prayer global community for a gathering in Madrid. We were worshiping with about a thousand friends from around forty different nations and it was glorious. Our reluctant leader, Pete Greig, began the entire conference by grabbing a chair and setting it on the stage. He said that the chair would remain there throughout every worship set, every teaching, and every workshop. It was a visual representation that Jesus was to remain front and center.

Sure, it's a chair. But something about the visual reminder of the centrality of Christ helped to steer every single gathering over the next few days. At one point, a couple of the other leaders invited Pete and his wife, Sammy, on stage. As soon as Pete realized that they were going to honor them publicly, he jumped off the stage, saying, "No! This will not be about me. The focus is to stay on Jesus." I do realize that honoring someone isn't wrong, and we certainly don't always need a chair on the stage, but that meeting ran in such contrast to some of the other church meetings I've attended. I believe that was because of the constant reminder of the centrality of Christ.

When Jesus is central, when He is glorified, when He is the focus of our full attention, the atmosphere changes. It is as if His DNA is present in

---

* Philippians 1:9-11 ESV

the room, and everything is different. The power of God did, indeed, pour forth in those meetings, and yet no one person could receive the credit. There wasn't a single "man of the hour" or "anointed one" that people exalted. We all walked away in awe of those days because of Jesus.

The way Jesus lived His life has everything to do with the prophetic. The way Jesus lived His life on earth has everything to do with everything. He is God's self-revelation on the earth. He is the meeting place of heaven and earth. All things are from Him, through Him, and for Him. Yahweh took on flesh and lived among us. How He chose to live His life in the flesh presents us with many complicated realities. What He did and didn't do, what He said and didn't say, and how He handled every situation before Him all has extreme significance. We imperfect yet eager followers of Jesus will grapple with the many dynamic implications of His life as long as we live. One thing I know for certain, is that we must begin every exploration about the prophetic by putting Jesus front and center, or we will be having the wrong conversation.

Remember, the purpose of the prophetic is to draw God's people into alignment with the covenant. In the Old Testament, the covenant was defined by the terms of the Law. In the New Testament, the covenant is Jesus, hence the reason why Revelation 19:10 says, "For the testimony of Jesus is the spirit of prophecy." Every prophetic word should draw our gaze, passion, desire, and Kingdom missions, ministries, etc., toward the person of Christ Jesus in Whom all eternal purposes reside.

This can look hundreds of different ways, of course, but the essence of every prophetic moment is to align with the eternal purposes of Christ. Period. Every single prophetic word, therefore, should be dripping with the DNA of Jesus. The words spoken, the actions demonstrated, the purpose of the words and actions themselves, and the spirit and character of the one speaking the words or doing the actions should all demonstrate, manifest, and embody the person of Jesus. This is not just a noble idea.

This looks like something. This feels like something, and this smells like something.

Sometimes it feels as if we treat the three years of Jesus' life and ministry as secondary. We focus on the cross and resurrection so intently (understandably so) that we subconsciously treat His life in the flesh as less important, as a warm-up act before the main event. Our Western mindset has a hard time understanding many of His actions, and it can wrongly seem as if He was just walking around healing people and teaching them the right way to live. But every single thing He did and said was prophetic in nature. His every word, action, and moment on earth were vital for our salvation and the establishment of the Kingdom. The incarnation itself is one of the most profound prophetic messages of all time, still preaching the intention of heaven into our lives today.

As Jesus lived out His sin-free life on earth inside of human flesh, breaking every barrier, tearing down every wall, conquering every shadow, and redeeming and restoring us every step of the way, He lived in perfect oneness with the Father. The King became one with His Creation and established His Kingdom on the earth. This is what the prophets declared, and it is what they lived for, what they pointed toward, and what everything in Scripture calls us to follow. This is why every recorded word and action of Jesus is vital for prophetic ministry today. He was the Prophet, and He still is. As Abraham Heschel said, "The Prophet is to represent God to the world, and the world to God."[12]

This is Jesus. To think that today's prophetic ministry in the New Testament Church wouldn't emanate His life, His character, His love, His truth, and His nature is wrong to the core. This looks like something. All prophetic ministry should spiritually echo who He is every single time. He is our hope of glory. He is the King of the Kingdom we serve. All things must point to Him, sound like Him, and carry His essence.

Throughout our entire Bible is the promise of a Prophet/King who will redeem His people.

"The LORD your God will raise up for you a prophet like me from among you, from your countrymen; to him you shall listen...And the LORD said to me, 'They have spoken well. I will raise up for them a prophet from among their countrymen like you, and I will put My words in his mouth, and he shall speak to them everything that I command him. And it shall come about that whoever does not listen to My words which he speaks in My name, I Myself will require it of him.'"*

The Old Testament predicted that God would raise up a prophet like Moses who would speak with God face to face. The New Testament claims that Jesus was the Prophet who was predicted in the Old Testament who would be like Moses and relate with God on a face-to-face basis. But Jesus was greater than Moses, for He was the one and only God who had eternally been face to face with the Father.

The Israelites held tightly to this promise and lived all their days watching and waiting for the Prophet who would be like Moses. This prophet would be different from the others. All the other prophets would speak words that pointed to this One. Hundreds of years went by, and still they watched and waited. At the time of Jesus' coming, the people were still looking for the Prophet. The religious leaders asked John the Baptist, "Are you the Prophet?"†

John said that he was not. He didn't deny that he was a prophetic voice, but He made it clear that he wasn't the Prophet for whom the people were waiting. When Jesus appeared on the scene and started performing miracles, He was recognized by many as the long-awaited prophet who was to come into the world. We know that He was much more than a prophet as He was truly God incarnate, but it's important to lean into the reality that

---

* Deuteronomy 18:15, 17-19
† John 1:21

He was also the prophet that all the Jews had been waiting for. "Therefore when the people saw the sign which He had performed, they said, 'This is truly the Prophet who is to come into the world.'"*

Jesus Himself testified that He was that prophet—the One who spoke the words from God the Father. "My teaching is not My own, but His who sent Me."† We need to understand what He was proclaiming to His Jewish audience as He spoke this sentence. He wasn't just saying, "Oh, God told me to say this." He was declaring for all of His Jewish listeners that He was the One for whom they had been waiting. He was the long-awaited Prophet, the redeemer, the Messiah. He spoke these kinds of things regularly and with great boldness.

Due to our Western mindset, we can miss the weighty significance of what He was proclaiming as he said things like:

"When you lift up the Son of Man, then you will know that I am, and I do nothing on My own, but I say these things as the Father instructed Me."‡

"For I did not speak on My own, but the Father Himself who sent Me has given Me a commandment as to what to say and what to speak. And I know that His commandment is eternal life; therefore the things I speak, I speak just as the Father has told me."§

"The one who does not love Me does not follow My words; and the word which you hear is not Mine, but the Father's who sent Me."¶

His claim was clear. He was, indeed, the Prophet for whom they had been waiting. This claim was bold, audacious, and politically charged with very serious repercussions.

---

*   John 6:14
†   John 7:16
‡   John 8:28
§   John 12:49-50
¶   John 14:24

What did the prophetic look like through Jesus? How can we learn from our primary prophetic mentor? It would take many, many books to even attempt to unpack all of the ways that Jesus prophesied, and I am dreadfully unqualified to do so. But let's lean into Matthew chapter 21 and look at three familiar stories.

I know this passage of Scripture is well known, but please take the time to read it slowly and imagine the story in your mind's eye as you read along.

When they had approached Jerusalem and had come to Bethphage, at the Mount of Olives, then Jesus sent two disciples, saying to them, "Go into the village opposite you, and immediately you will find a donkey tied there and a colt with her; untie them and bring them to Me. If anyone says anything to you, you shall say, 'The Lord has need of them,' and immediately he will send them." This took place to fulfill what was spoken through the prophet:

"Say to the daughter of zion, 'behold your king is coming to you, gentle, and mounted on a donkey, even on a colt, the foal of a beast of burden.'"[*]

The disciples went and did just as Jesus had instructed them, and brought the donkey and the colt, and laid their coats on them; and He sat on the coats. Most of the crowd spread their coats in the road, and others were cutting branches from the trees and spreading them in the road. The crowds going ahead of Him, and those who followed, were shouting,

"Hosanna to the Son of David;

blessed is he who comes in the name of the lord;

Hosanna in the highest!"[†]

---

[*] Matthew 21:5
[†] Matthew 21:9

When He had entered Jerusalem, all the city was stirred, saying "Who is this?" And the crowds were saying, "This is the prophet Jesus, from Nazareth in Galilee."*

Let's place ourselves inside the experience of the Jewish followers of Jesus. Imagine being on that fateful road and cheering His ride into town on what we now call Palm Sunday. What would we be thinking? What would we be expecting? What would we be feeling? This is a massive turning point in the story of Jesus. Until now, He had attempted to stay under the radar. At this moment, however, He went radically public.

It was Passover week in Jerusalem. There are normally 50,000 residents in the city; however, an extra 150,000 people visited this city during Passover. The streets would have been massively crowded. Jesus chose this moment to take His ministry public. He chose this day, this hour and this feast to make His entrance. We Westerners wouldn't instinctively see the symbolic nature of His donkey ride, but every Jew in the city on this holiday weekend would understand automatically.

King David had entered Jerusalem on a donkey on the same road (2 Samuel 16). This happened as he was being reinstated as Israel's king. Solomon did the same thing. On the way to his coronation, Solomon rode his father's donkey on the same road (1 Kings 1:38). To these crowds, the act would not have gone unnoticed. Jesus was declaring that He would be King. He intentionally and publicly presented Himself as King, and the people responded by demonstrating their faith in who He was. The crowds shouted hosanna, which means "save me." They cried out for Jesus to save them, proving that they believed He was the Messiah, that He was the long-awaited Prophet.

It also could be seen as an act of war, as Jerusalem already had leaders. The chief priests and the Sanhedrin were the religious leaders, and Caesar

---

*   Matthew 21:1-9

was the Emperor of the Roman empire. The people would have seen Jesus' entry into Jerusalem as a clear declaration that He was challenging the powers that currently led His people. The Jews would not have missed the significance of His actions. Neither would the Romans.

Since His entrance wasn't followed up with a violent takeover or a public coronation, this would have been very confusing for the Jews. The Roman leaders did not step aside and give Jesus the throne. They crucified Him instead. Was this devastating for the Jewish people? You bet. They believed that Jesus was the Prophet, the Messiah, and they were likely waving those palm branches believing that the violent takeover was about to begin. N. T. Wright wrote,

He was not the king they expected. He wasn't like the monarchs of old who sat on their jeweled and ivory thrones, dispensing their justice and wisdom. Nor was he the great warrior-king some had wanted. He didn't raise an army and ride into battle at its head. He was riding on a donkey. And he was weeping, weeping for the dream that had to die, weeping for the sword that would pierce his supporters to the soul. Weeping for the kingdom that wasn't coming as well as for the kingdom that was.[13]

What happens next?

When He had entered Jerusalem, all the city was stirred, saying, "Who is this?" And the crowds were saying, "This is the prophet, Jesus, from Nazareth in Galilee." And Jesus entered the temple and drove out all those who were buying and selling in the temple, and overturned the tables of the money changers and the seats of those who were selling doves. And He said to them, "It is written, 'MY HOUSE SHALL BE CALLED A HOUSE OF PRAYER'; but you are making it a ROBBERS' DEN." And the blind and the lame came to Him in the temple, and He healed them. But when the chief priests and the scribes saw the wonderful things that He had done, and the children who were shouting in the temple, "Hosanna to the Son of David," they became indignant and said to Him, "Do You hear what these children are saying?" And Jesus said to them, "Yes; have you never read, 'OUT OF THE MOUTH OF INFANTS AND NURSING BABIES YOU HAVE PREPARED PRAISE FOR YOURSELF'?" And He left them and went out of the city to Bethany, and spent the night there (Matthew 21:10-17).

In verse 10, we see a word that is translated as stirred. This word often means "utter chaos."[14] Imagine hundreds of people filling the streets, with heightened excitement and tension, due to the arrival of Jesus. It may have felt akin to a revolution! The atmosphere must have been a mixture of elation, anger, passion, division and fear. Then, to make matters even more intense, Jesus stirs things up further. The words drove out that we see in verse 12 mean "with a strong violence."[15] This was not a calm act. Amid utter chaos, that probably felt like an uprising, Jesus makes a rope (John 2:13-16). He then gets to work violently, passionately, and intentionally storming the temple and flipping tables. This isn't a random, uncontrolled act. This is purposeful and prophetic.

Take note of the specifics mentioned: the tables of the money-changers and the seats of those selling doves. If you could not afford a lamb, you were permitted to buy a dove to offer instead (Leviticus 5:7). The doves, therefore, were the offering of the poor. So when Jesus turns over the seats of those who were selling the doves, He is defending the poor. This facet of the story is mentioned specifically and intentionally. The words He speaks in verse 13 seem to be directed toward those who were selling the doves. This is true in John's account as well (John 2:13-16).

The words that Jesus quotes in verse 13 combine two Old Testament prophetic utterances. One came from Isaiah 56:7. Isaiah gave direct instructions that the Israelites were to receive the foreigner and welcome the outcast. Jesus, however, witnessed the poor being taken advantage of and barriers being put in place to keep the foreigners from worship. The other reference came from Jeremiah's condemnation of divided hearts who gloss over sin and then stand presumptuously before the Lord as if there is nothing wrong (Jeremiah 7:11). His message seems clear, and the people witnessing these acts most likely understood what He was communicating

As you read the words below, can you imagine yourself inside this event? Imagine standing nearby, watching Jesus as He runs through the temple flipping those tables:

> *I watch You enter*
> *This sacred space*
> *Your face is contorted*
>
> *Your anguish*
> *Is emanating*
> *As Your cries echo*
> *Off these temple walls*
>
> *What's gripping You?*
> *I need to know. What's arresting You*
> *As you flip those tables?*
>
> *What do You see*
> *That we cannot see?*
> *What causes you such pain?*
> *We need to know*
>
> *You could have grabbed a pulpit*
> *And explained what was wrong*
> *You could have held a meeting*
> *And spoke to the matter at hand*

But You didn't.
You won't.
You're confronting
Opposing
Violently
Upending

The anguish
oh… The anguish
Just looking at You is painful
This isn't about the tables

You're seeing something
We cannot see.
You're living for something
We cannot see.
You're dying for something
We cannot see.

So we talk about the tables.
We analyze the tables.
We discuss the tables.
And we try to move on.

Did they return the next day
And fix those broken legs?
Did they have a meeting
To talk about new tables?
Someone had to clean up
The mess You made.

Who were the ones who
Sensed Your broken dream?
Who felt Your agony
And trembled?

Who were the ones
Who didn't look away?
Who opened themselves
And welcomed the undoing?

Help us, oh Tortured One
To sense what moves You
Help us, Afflicted One
To feel what pulls You

To glimpse the promise
To smell the garden
To taste the dream
And ache over the chasm
In between

Please, oh Sacred One
Turn over our tables
And don't stop
Upend us
Over and over
Until we see
Until we dream Your dream

Directly after Jesus flips those tables, this is the story we read, "Now in the morning when He was returning to the city, He became hungry. Seeing a lone fig tree by the road, He came to it and found nothing on it except leaves only; and He said to it, 'No longer shall there ever be any fruit from you.' And at once the fig tree withered. Seeing this, the disciples were amazed and asked, 'How did the fig tree wither all at once?' And Jesus answered and said to them, 'Truly I say to you, if you have faith and do not doubt, you will not only do what was done to the fig tree, but even if you say to this mountain, 'Be taken up and cast into the sea,' it will happen. And all things you ask in prayer, believing, you will receive.'"*

Here is this seemingly random moment where Jesus curses the fig tree. Is He just mad at the fig tree for not giving Him food because He is hungry? No. There are half a dozen times in the Old Testament where Israel is compared to a fig tree. This is a prophetic moment. Read Micah 3:9-12 and Micah 7:1-4 for examples. The metaphor between the fruitfulness of a fig tree is compared to Israel's spiritual fruitfulness throughout the Old Testament. They often described God as inspecting Israel for "early figs" for a sign of growth.

"When I would gather them, declares the LORD, there are no grapes on the vine, nor figs on the fig tree; even the leaves are withered, and what I gave them has passed away from them."†

In two exiles, God puts the curse of barrenness upon them for their rejection of Him, and Israel becomes a rotten fig. Yet, God in His mercy promises to one day replant Israel and produce healthy figs from her again (Joel 2:22; Amos 9:14; Micah 4:4; Zech. 8:12; Ezekiel 36:8). Every good Jew knew all of this, and they would have understood what Jesus was saying in this moment.

---

*   Matthew 21:18-22
†   Jeremiah 8:13 ESV

Jesus had just ridden the meaning-laden donkey into town, hailed Himself as King, and cleansed the temple in a dramatic demonstration as the Passover festivities were in full swing. There was a lot of spiritual activity that was happening without righteousness. Jesus enters God's house of prayer and finds it a "den of robbers," like leaves without fruit. Yet when the disciples ask Jesus to explain, He seems to pivot and begin teaching them about prayer. Is it because these disciples will be the new caretakers of God's people? They will be the ones to carry the Good News to the nations. They don't know it yet, but soon they will face mountains of religious persecution, and they will remember this moment. Jesus was simultaneously prophesying over Israel and prophesying over His disciples.

So, where do we go from here? Seeing these stories in what may be a new light may also cause you to see a different side of Jesus than you have seen before. Learning from Jesus as the Prophet, as the revelation of God in the world, must have an impact on how we view the prophetic. His prophetic acts point somewhere. They communicate something, and they are in line with His eternal purposes. Jesus is our Lord, our King, our Savior, and our Love. If our prophetic words do not emanate His character, His beauty, His purposes, and His ways, they are not genuinely prophetic. Period.

He is patient, kind, is not arrogant, does not act unbecomingly, is not provoked, does not take into account a wrong suffered, and does not rejoice in unrighteousness but rejoices with the truth. He bears all things, believes all things, hopes all things, and endures all things. He is in us, and we are in Him. We have been crucified with Him. It is no longer we who live but Christ who lives in us. We are partakers of His divine nature. This is true of all believers, of course. So it most certainly should be true of our modern-day prophetic ministry.

There's a rumbling under the surface within every page of this holy book.

> *The relentless, determined unveiling of Yahweh*
> *Beats like a heart-pounding between every line.*
> *God's unwavering pursuit is seen within every story,*
> *Every prophecy, every word,*
> *Exposing His eternal longing*
> *To be known.*
> *He made humans in His own Image*
> *To be known.*
> *He pulled back the curtain of heaven for a humble, stuttering Moses*
> *To be known.*
> *He stood on the mount of transfiguration revealing His glory.*
> *He ushered Isaiah, Ezekiel and John into His Throne Room*
> *So their eyes would see and*
> *Their ears would hear*
> *the "Holy, holy, holy,"*
> *To be known.*
> *He took on flesh to reflect His nature*
> *To a watching world.*
> *"This is eternal life, that they may know You."**
> *Every prophetic moment is a returning*
> *To righteousness, to covenant, to relationship,*
> *To Jesus.*
> *If the prophetic testifies,*
> *If the prophetic declares,*
> *If the prophetic points to Jesus,*
> *Then maybe we shouldn't just study the prophetic.*
> *We should study Jesus.*
> *He dines with the distasteful.*
> *He defends the adulterous.*
> *He feeds the hungry, loves the children, and cries over those in pain.*
> *He is both holy and majestic and incredibly kind and gentle.*
> *His humility is unfathomable.*

---

*   John 17:3

He washes His followers' feet!
He interrupts religious ceremonies to heal a withered hand.
He turned over tables without fear of judgment.
Passion for His Father's house was His obsession.
He brought dignity to women in a culture that treated them like dogs.
He held the leper in His arms,
He adored the outcast,
The rejected,
The diseased,
The unclean.
He pursued the detested,
He held the rejected,
Touched the untouchable.
Those who were shamed found acceptance.
Those who were hated found love.
This Jesus IS the prophetic Word of God.
"The Son is the radiance of God's glory and the exact representation of
his being, sustaining all things by his powerful word."
The invitation is scandalous.
It is shocking to the senses.
We are invited into this Jesus.
"For in Him we live and move and have our being."†
This is our call…
He's on a mission, and we're invited.
"God utters me like a word containing a partial thought of Himself."16
Stand before His Throne, my friends!
Draw near to the fire of the Holy.
Fall on your knees,
Behold Him,
Reveal Him.
"The witness of Jesus is the very breath of prophecy."‡
He is the Word made flesh.

This is a study of Jesus.

---

*   Hebrews 1:3 NIV
†   Acts 17:28 NIV
‡   Revelation 19:10

— CHAPTER 5 —

Prophets and Artists

"All the prophets were poets" is a phrase we've heard from the likes of Eugene Peterson, Dr. Ellen Davis at Fuller, as well as many other theologians, artists, and poets. It could be said that all the prophets were artists, not just poets. Several prophets, including Abraham, Moses, Ahijah, Elijah, Isaiah, Deborah, Jeremiah, Ezekiel, and Jesus used symbolic actions—without words—to prophesy. Their creative demonstration, action, gesture, movement, or posture was an artistic approach to communicating vital messages to the people. It could be argued that a large part of God's interaction with Moses on the mountain for forty days might have included intricate instructions for the artwork within the temple that would prophetically point to the redemption of Christ.

To remove art from the prophets would mean removing the prophets themselves. One-third of the Bible is poetry, one-third of the Bible is prose. Removing poetry, prose, and artistic, prophetic demonstration from the Bible would leave scattered fragments behind. So we must ask ourselves why the arts, especially poetry, are often marginalized in our culture, especially within the walls of many of our churches. I'm sure there are several ways to answer that question, not the least of which would be to point toward the Greek mindset in the West that exalts knowledge over creativity.

So if all the prophets were poets, the flipside must also be considered. I'm not saying that all the poets in the world are prophets, but I am saying that I believe there are many, many poets, sculptors, dancers, musicians, and actors who truly are prophets and may not know it. Most of them certainly wouldn't know where they could possibly fit within our churches.

Let's take a look at David. We often think of David as a king, a worshiper, a warrior, or a poet, but rarely is he referred to as a prophet. Yet David shares more Messianic prophecies than any other prophet in Scripture. Often, in the middle of his lament, his poetry, or his praise, he pens seemingly cryptic or even off-topic sentences that end up being fulfilled very precisely in the life, death, and resurrection of Christ. I don't think it is far-fetched to say that the Psalms are hugely responsible for us being able to recognize Jesus as the Messiah.

So, if this book is about observing the prophetic in Scripture, then we must take a good look at the personality of the prophetic in the songs, lament, poetry, and worship found in the book of Psalms. Truth be told, if we look at David's prophetic credentials, we could say that the book of Psalms should be one of the primary places in which we should study the prophetic.

The prophetic within the arts is not a new conversation. Many people in today's world discuss prophetic art, but I have found that most of these conversations barely scratch the surface. How do artists prophesy? What is their experience as the Holy Spirit moves through them? How do they relate to the Church at large? How do they influence the local church?

David painted pictures with his words. He prayed violently with his words. He lamented passionately, honestly, and vulnerably through his words, and his words were his art. And his art was often intensely prophetic.

"When we discuss the prophetic in the Psalms, it's important that we begin with the right set of questions. Whenever you go to a text, you are asking questions about it. If it's a science book, we read with certain questions in our minds. If it's a religious text, we have a set of questions we are bringing with us to the text, whether we're aware of them or not. When we open the Scripture, we usually have specific, immediate life, morality, or spiritual growth questions. As we approach the Psalms, what questions do we have in our minds and hearts? What if I approach the Psalms the same way I would slowly wander through an art gallery? In this way, I'm exploring the deeper meaning within the art rather than looking for facts or information. This is a different heart stance altogether, and it changes the way we receive the words." ~ Joe Spann, poet and elder at Believers Church, Tulsa OK.

As we read the book of Psalms as a piece of art, we notice certain things that help reframe the prophetic. The first thing we need to note is that these poems are carefully crafted works of art. They were not sudden eruptions of emotion or spontaneous ecstatic prophecies. The author uses rhyme schemes, metaphors, syllabic patterns, words to fit melodies, etc. They had to be crafted, well thought out, edited, and cultivated. When we overemphasize ecstatic experience, we can wrongfully use this to validate that we heard from the Lord. A heavily emotional experience of God's presence can be powerful, indeed, but we should never use this as proof of authorization. Suppose we use an adrenaline rush as the criteria that God is speaking. If we do, we might miss the expansiveness of the contemplative, prophetic artist who usually hears, sees, and awakens to the voice of God gradually and gently.

When you take time to ponder the depth in which a poet relates with the voice of God as they search for the exact words the Spirit wants to use to communicate, you can begin to see the importance of time. Poets need time to allow the creative process to churn within them slowly. They often carry inspiration in the same way that a pregnant mother has a growing child in her womb. They grapple over various words and metaphors to try to communicate the expanse of the message from the Father to whoever will listen.

It is the same with painters, sculptors, musicians, dancers, etc. Each of these artists would most often tell you that they have a message they carry within themselves—not just a picture or a song, but a message they want to communicate. This message needs to grow, evolve, and take shape over time. Eventually, they will slowly and painstakingly give birth to how they want to communicate. It will take much time and meticulous attention to every detail. Often, they don't understand the why of the message or for whom it may specifically be. They just know it must come into being.

I think about this often as I read the Psalms, and I wonder why God chose David to drop the most extensive popcorn trail that led to Jesus. Something about the artist's message engages the receiver's heart and soul more deeply. They don't spoon-feed us information by giving us facts and instructions. They express something from heaven that calls us to look beyond the obvious. We, therefore, pause, reflect, and invite the Holy Spirit to speak to us through their creativity. There's an intimacy that art pulls us into that is unique and to be cherished by us all.

Artists "hear the 'music of the spheres' and desire to respond; they see a vista beyond the world of gray utility; they desire to paint in color; they dance to a tune of the Maker who leads us beyond restoration into the New World to come."[17] The heart and mind of the artist is prophetic at the root. All art points somewhere. When surrendered to the Holy Spirit, His presence will guide the process as He co-creates with His son or daughter, often pointing to the New Creation Kingdom. Co-creating with God is the invitation to us all, whether or not we consider ourselves artists. The Master Artist takes great joy in creating! He has never stopped creating, and His constant bidding draws us into the adventure of co-creating with Him every day.

We co-create with God when we love, forgive, and show mercy. Our every act on this earth creates. While we might talk of our gifts and calling, we often discuss these things framed in a pragmatic utilitarianism that can strip away beauty and intimacy. We have a deeply ingrained cultural value of purpose, progress, and accomplishment, which can sometimes hinder our understanding of the power of beauty. But God is a Creator who longs to create beauty in the earth, with His sons and daughters.

We can learn so much from the way artists live and breathe the message of God. Many of them live in such a way that they are almost constantly pregnant with a partially formed revelation of beauty, the pain and brokenness of our world, or a longing of what could be. They are often holding something within their soul for weeks, months, or years at a time, well before they put their hands to the creating process.

This is similar to many prophets who walk around with a partially formed message from heaven rumbling within them. They seem to search for the missing pieces throughout their every moment, looking for God around every corner, seeking His presence within every mundane moment of their day.

Many prophetically gifted people can find themselves holding something in their spirit that isn't clear (yet) in their minds. Even so, it reverberates through their entire body day after day, gradually taking shape. For many prophetic voices, myself included, this has become a way of life. Even though I'm not artistically gifted, I relate to the artist's process because it feels familiar with how the Holy Spirit leads me. I often feel like a pregnant woman walking around with something from heaven forming within me that is still growing and taking shape, ever-so-slowly.

"As the child growing in the womb changes the mother before it enters the world, the inspiration stirring first changes the artist."[18] The same is often true of the prophet. When we allow the message of the Lord to grow gradually within us, we are transformed by His voice. Through this process, we hopefully become the person He needs to deliver the message.

Learning how to remain in the tension of carrying an incomplete message takes quite a long time. It is uncomfortable, to say the least, because we can often feel the emotions of the word before the words are present. Or we can sense the intercession of the Holy Spirit burning within us, and all we can do is groan. Yet, we also know there is a message from heaven in it all, and it burns in our bones way before the Lord releases us to bring it forth. When you can see what the Holy Spirit is doing within you, you can fully surrender to the journey and allow it to be a profoundly intimate space with you and the Lord. He's forming the words within you and transforming you into the messenger He desires.

People often teach that knowing the right time to share a prophetic word is essential. This is true, of course, but it feels a little two-dimensional for my taste. The process is more than just learning when to jump, speak, or keep quiet. The Lord invites us to carry His desire within our spirit, allowing it to imprint upon our heart, changing us forever. If we remain in union with Him throughout this process, timing won't be an issue. This process requires patience, silence, and stamina.

Patience and silence become our intimate friends as we learn to wait and surrender to the Holy Spirit's movement within. We know that we are not just waiting for words to speak, but we are cultivating an awareness of His heart, desire, and intention. We must learn how to slow down and lean into His movement with our whole being. We need stamina because we too quickly become distracted and give up. It takes nine months for new life to mature within the womb. Can you imagine if we decided that pregnancy took too long and we tried to rush the process?

We have a patience problem in our culture, this much we know. We need to learn the art of daily searching. Our instant gratification has wounded the beauty of longing, and it is truly devastating. Longing is the soil that cultivates new life. As we look around at the natural world, we realize that nothing grows instantly. Why do we expect the prophetic to be instantaneous?

My artist friends will compare this experience to their constant search for a muse. They search for beauty with an almost desperate need to find God within everything they see. They search for His presence in leaves on a tree, a cracked sidewalk, or a lost soul holding a sign on the side of the road. They're longing for the revelation of His beauty, and it doesn't matter where or how they find it. They feel this unformed, incomplete message from heaven rumbling and churning over and over within them, and they learn to hold it tenderly as they search for its maturing voice. They search and search, looking with different eyes than the rest of us, hearing with different ears than most, and finding His glory everywhere they look.

As David penned, "The heavens declare the glory of God; the skies proclaim the work of his hands."* you can hear his longing. We hear agony, questions, and a churning heart throughout David's writing. But within the Psalms, how is the prophetic communicated? Can we see how the prophetic moves through David as we observe his art? Sometimes a whole psalm prophesies Christ, such as Psalm 22.

Sometimes we see just a paragraph of Messianic prophecies, such as in Psalm 40:6-10. Other times, we will see several verses that seem more scattered, such as in Psalm 69:4,9, and 21. For the sake of this study and to observe the prophetic in action, let's lean into Psalm 22 (verses 1,2,7,8,12-19) and then make comparisons to Matthew 27.

"My God, my God, why have You forsaken me?
Far from my deliverance are the words of my groaning.
O my God, I cry by day, but You do not answer;
And by night, but I have no rest."

---

*   Psalm 19:1 NIV

"All who see me sneer at me;

They separate with the lip, they wag the head, saying,

"Commit yourself to the LORD; let Him deliver him;

Let Him rescue him, because He delights in him."

"Many bulls have surrounded me;

Strong bulls of Bashan have encircled me.

They open wide their mouth at me,

As a ravening and a roaring lion.

I am poured out like water,

And all my bones are out of joint;

My heart is like wax;

It is melted within me.

My strength is dried up like a potsherd,

And my tongue cleaves to my jaws;

And You lay me in the dust of death.

For dogs have surrounded me;

A band of evildoers has encompassed me;

They pierced my hands and my feet.

I can count all my bones.

They look, they stare at me;

They divide my garments among them,

And for my clothing they cast lots.

But You, O LORD, be not far off;"

The more we lean into the possible experiences of David, the more we find questions stirring that are unanswerable. We must learn to soak within the questions, allowing space for joyful curiosity to express itself. Wonder can create a space within our hearts and minds for more profound glimpses into the character of God.

One of the beautiful things that art calls forth in our souls is the language of mystery. The arts give language to a question without needing to have the answer. Wisdom learns how to hold the questions in tension—in wonder. Our intellect wants the answers. Our modern-day mindsets want the answers. But the heart of an artist searches for the beautification of the question. Our Western culture is fiercely uncomfortable with mystery. Just think of how we would squirm if a cord during a worship set was left unresolved, or how we may tilt in confusion listening to poetry that doesn't spell things out with cliches. True art should not be immediately understood. It requires time, and the kind of looking and listening that goes beyond the surface. Mystery was a fundamental way of knowing the unknowable for the early Christian mothers and fathers. Today, our way of life is rooted in utilitarianism, and that mindset struggles against the deeper places that art longs to invite us into. As we lean into the beauty of the prophetic arts, it is important that we honor the words that are not spoken. If we try to explain everything and fill in all the empty spaces, we will tragically over-simplify the depth and complexity of meaning.

As David penned this psalm, what did he know, and what did he not know? Did he know that this would be a literal event that would happen a thousand years later, just as he described? What may have been David's experience as the Holy Spirit moved through him to pen these words? What understanding may he have had at the moment? When did clarity concerning this prophetic psalm come, if at all? As we imagine David writing this psalm, we also can see how Jesus related to and fulfilled these words a thousand years later.

As we turn to Matthew 27:27-46 and pay attention to how the words of David from Psalm 22 appeared as a record in the witnesses of the death of Christ, we can put a couple of pieces together, but only slightly.

Then the soldiers of the governor took Jesus into the Praetorium and gathered the whole Roman cohort around Him. They stripped Him and put a scarlet robe on Him. And after twisting together a crown of thorns, they put it on His head, and a reed in His right hand; and they knelt down before Him and mocked Him, saying, "Hail, King of the Jews!" They spat on Him, and took the reed and began to beat Him on the head. After they had mocked Him, they took the scarlet robe off Him and put His own garments back on Him, and led Him away to crucify Him. As they were coming out, they found a man of Cyrene named Simon, whom they pressed into service to bear His cross. And when they came to a place called Golgotha, which means Place of a Skull, they gave Him wine to drink mixed with gall; and after tasting it, He was unwilling to drink. And when they had crucified Him, they divided up His garments among themselves by casting lots. And sitting down, they began to keep watch over Him there. And above His head, they put up the charge against Him, which read, "THIS IS JESUS THE KING OF THE JEWS." At that time, two robbers *were crucified with Him, one on the right and one on the left. And those passing by were hurling abuse at Him, wagging their heads and saying, "You who are going to destroy the temple and rebuild it in three days, save Yourself! If You are the Son of God, come down from the cross." In the same way, the chief priests, along with the scribes and elders, mocked Him, saying, "He saved others; He cannot save Himself. He is the King of Israel; let Him now come down from the cross, and we will believe in Him. HE TRUSTS IN GOD; LET GOD RESCUE Him now, IF HE DELIGHTS IN HIM; for He said, 'I am the Son of God.'" The robbers who had been crucified with Him were also insulting Him with the same words. Now from the sixth hour darkness fell upon all the land until the ninth hour. About the ninth hour Jesus cried out with a loud voice, saying, "ELI, ELI, LAMA SABACHTHANI?" that is, "MY GOD, MY GOD, WHY HAVE YOU FORSAKEN ME?"

If you're like me, you have a million questions running through your head right now. Were the Jewish witnesses of this moment familiar with this psalm of David? Did they connect the moment they were seeing with their eyes to the words of the psalmist a thousand years earlier? Did David see this moment as he crafted those words in Psalm 22? What did David feel as he wrote? Did God pull back the veil for David to glimpse this moment from heaven's perspective, or was he just gently following the Holy Spirit and writing words that made no logical sense to him at the time? Did he look at this poem and think he must be crazy?

As we allow the wonder of it all to grow within our hearts, even though we don't have concrete answers, walls begin to break down in our thinking. Curiosity is so helpful in dismantling our modern-day cultural views. We often feel afraid to ask these kinds of questions because we want to feel in control. But as we learn to let the questions remain without having to find answers, we give the Holy Spirit space to awaken a more biblical imagination.

Makoto Fujimura shares in his book Art and Faith:

> Christians have many presuppositions about what Christianity is that are often based upon an analytical approach to understanding truth as a set of propositional beliefs, such that understanding and explaining take dominance over experiencing and intuiting. But that grounding is based less on a biblical, generative path than on the mechanistic, postindustrial thinking of utilitarian pragmatism. Imagine trying to explain to a flying bird the aerodynamic forces at work when its wings move. Perhaps explaining it undermines the flight itself; perhaps the effort to understand it will not help the flying at all.[19]

Our Western mindsets want to force the prophetic to be clearly understood, with action steps and full explanations. There is nowhere in Scripture that we see the prophetic work this way.

Some churches create space for painters or dancers to express their gifts during worship, which is a beautiful step in a good direction. Yet, there is so much more work to be done. Do these artists, dancers, singers, and musicians understand the true prophetic? Are they taught the difference between a spontaneous expression of worship and a prophetic message from God? Have we taught the congregation how to relate to art that may carry a prophetic message? This would take much rewiring of our deeply rooted expectations of learning. Most of us do not have ears to hear or eyes to see what the Holy Spirit may be speaking through the artists unless it's very obvious and often propagandistic. "You can make art about the Light, or you can make art that shows what the Light reveals about the world."[20]

The Sunday morning context also puts a great deal of pressure on artists to fit within our paradigm of ecstatic spontaneity. Most gifted artists could find this type of expectation a near violation of the way they experience the Holy Spirit intimately creating through them. Most artists still don't see where their gift fits within the local church. One reason may be that we have boxed much of our prophetic expression into a Sunday morning worship service or a prayer meeting. If the prophetic can truly function similarly to what we see in the New Testament, then it must break out of the Sunday box.

Sure, there may be times the Lord speaks through a prophetic person during a worship service, but this is only one small way the prophetic relates to the local church. There are painters, dancers, sculptors, actors, and poets who are true prophets, but they have no idea how to bring their gift to the Church. So many of them have left the building, per se, and taken their gifting to the world. Of course, this isn't a bad thing because the world needs their gifts. God can and will speak through their creations no matter where they are, whether or not they are in the faith, aware or unaware. But I believe the Church is malnourished without this particular food group, and it's a tragedy that we aren't receiving the messages the Lord wants to speak through them.

Our vision must expand. Our understanding of the prophetic through the arts must grow, or we will continue to suffer extreme loss. If we minimize the prophetic to the spontaneous, in-the-moment revelation shared in the middle of a worship service, then we are those who would have missed David's popcorn trail to the Messiah. If we only see the prophetic as encouraging words between individuals, we are altogether discounting the purpose of the prophetic.

What is keeping us from fully receiving the prophetic artists in our churches? We undoubtedly have mindsets that need changing and systems that need confronting. One of which could be our drive for accomplishment and advancement, which in and of itself isn't a bad thing. We live in a Christian culture that has the strengths and weaknesses of the utilitarian efficiency that has helped accomplish amazing things, such as international missions movements and evangelistic initiatives.

Yet the downside of this efficiency is that it can be damaging to artists. There is nothing about the prophetic and art in general that will thrive within an efficiency-oriented, fast-paced culture. Artists and prophets alike thrive within spaciousness. We flourish in uncluttered solitude and the expansive breath of unscheduled days. There have been a lot of discussions lately about the value of the Sabbath, rest, silence, and solitude. I can't help but wonder if the Lord is trying to guide our culture to make room for the prophets (and artists) to arise.

I'm sure we could quickly list some of the most obvious hindrances to having eyes to see all the ways He is speaking. What if we gathered artists together into prophetic communities, helped them see how they relate to the Holy Spirit through their gift, and truly validated the message they were carrying? What if we helped them see through Scripture why they are so important to the Body of Christ and where they fit? What if we dreamt of ways to receive their gift that would help us to hear God's voice in new ways?

When the prophetic is standing in its rightful, healthy place, the Church will receive the guidance that the prophetic brings, regardless of whether it comes through someone like John the Baptist or someone more like David. We need eyes to see and ears to hear where He is speaking, how

He is speaking, and through whom He is speaking. We desperately need the gift and perspective of artists.

Christy Tennant, director of Global Community for International Arts Movement, has written a beautiful article on prophetic artists. In this article, she asks the questions most of us are asking.

> We ask our painters to adorn the children's wing of our churches, we commission singable worship tunes, we ask our graphic artists to create bulletin templates, and we invite actors to perform skits before the pastor takes the stage to bring the "real" message. But where is the prophetic function of art in this? As I consider the prophetically inspired arts found in Jeremiah and Ezekiel, I wonder, What would happen if, on occasion, preachers invited the artists among them to interpret God's word through their art and let that art be the sermon? Not as a warm-up to the sermon, but as the sermon itself?[21]

— CHAPTER 6 —

Acts

A few years ago, I was struggling deeply with some unhealthy and damaging prophetic words that were flying around. So one night, I sat down a bit half-heartedly and opened the book of Acts. As I read, I was searching for the prophetic in action. I needed to see it in motion. Within a couple of pages, I felt suddenly alert, as if I had stumbled into a gold mine. I have read the stories in Acts many times before, but this time, I was reading with different eyes. I was looking for the Spirit of Prophecy as He clothed Himself in various people and places.

It felt as if I was watching a character in a movie who took on different personas, but the DNA was the same every time He appeared. The more I read and underlined, the more in awe I became by what I was seeing. It took an hour or so, but at the end of it, I closed my Bible, sat back in my chair, and allowed the shock waves to move through me.

After many years of teaching and preaching on the prophetic, I had never leaned in more deeply to see the Spirit of Prophecy in action throughout Acts. Embarrassingly enough, I had never even seen these stories as examples of prophecy. I found myself both exhilarated and sick to my stomach. I was exhilarated because I felt as if I saw the purpose of the prophetic more clearly than ever. I was sick to my stomach because

I now had to reconcile the way the prophetic looked in our modern-day Western culture.

In all the ways I had experienced the prophetic, I can honestly say it never looked like what I had just seen in the unfolding of the Great Commission. This threw me into months of deep study, through which I came to one pretty firm conclusion: when it comes to the root systems of the prophetic in many cultures today, we don't have a gift problem, we have a purpose problem. What I mean is that many people have powerful gifts from the Holy Spirit. There are people in the Body of Christ that are gifted at hearing the voice of God, or sensing what the Holy Spirit may be doing. But it seems that in many expressions of charismatic prophetic ministry, we have lost sight of the purpose of the prophetic. As the old adage goes, if you don't know the purpose of a thing, you are destined to abuse it.

I know that you might be citing 1 Corinthians 14:3 to me: "But he who prophesies speaks edification and exhortation and comfort to men." This has been the most common understanding in the Western world of the purpose of the New Testament prophetic. I would challenge this with two thoughts. The first one is that the words edification, exhortation, and comfort pretty much cover everything. It is too easy for us to read those words and presume that we know what the writer was referring to. This has been interpreted in many circles as meaning that every prophetic word needs to make people feel good. This is not what this passage of Scripture is talking about.

The second is that we in Western culture have made comfort a pretty massive idol. We do love our comfort! Is it possible that we have read this passage through the lens of our cultural idol and then made presumptions about what it means? I'm pretty sure Paul thought he was being very edifying to the Galatians when he said:

"I am astonished that you are so quickly deserting him who called you in the grace of Christ and are turning to a different gospel not that there is another one, but there are some who trouble you and want to distort the gospel of Christ. But even if we or an angel from heaven should preach to you a gospel contrary to the one we preached to you, let him be accursed. As we have said before, so now I say again: If anyone is preaching to you a gospel contrary to the one you received, let him be accursed."*

Taking what Paul wrote in this passage and running it through our modern-day cultural filters could most definitely cause a distortion in our understanding. I really love the idea that all prophecy is to make us feel good and happy. It feels safer, especially to the pastorally-minded ones among us.

But, as I read through the book of Acts, I saw the purpose of the prophetic loud and clear in a way I had never seen before. I saw the Spirit of Prophecy on an obvious mission. It wasn't random. The emotional state of humans didn't drive it. It wasn't on a stage, at a conference, or wowing people with the impressive things it knew about someone. This Spirit of Prophecy was pointing somewhere. It was accomplishing something very specific and headed in one obvious direction.

I encourage you to do this exercise for yourself. Set aside a couple of hours to skim through the whole book of Acts, with pen in hand, underlining every moment that feels prophetic in nature. Take note of Jesus telling the disciples that the Holy Spirit would come and baptize them all and that they should wait in the city for this to happen.

Pay attention to Jesus telling them that once the Holy Spirit had come upon them, they would "be My witnesses both in Jerusalem, and in all Judea and Samaria, and even to the remotest part of the earth."† This is Jesus prophesying. He is giving instructions simultaneously and foretelling

---

*   Galatians 1:6-9 ESV
†   Acts 1:8

what will happen. This is God's hand of direction leading the events that needed to unfold to see the birth of the Church spring into being.

Make sure you underline the moment when two men in white clothing prophesy to the stunned disciples that, "This Jesus, who has been taken up from you into heaven, will come in just the same way as you have watched him go into heaven."* They not only give the disciples a bit of a nudge out of their shock, but they prophesy the return of Christ.

I suggest that you grab a different color highlighter and note when the people in the story refer back to an Old Testament prophecy to help make sense of their current situation. These are equally important lessons as we observe how these Jewish brothers and sisters related to the prophetic. Watching the way these early believers relied on prophetic words to anchor them, direct them, and interpret the happenings of heaven in their midst is instructive for us today.

As you get to the end of Acts, I hope you find that you have highlighted something prophetic on nearly every page. The prophetic was instrumental within every single step of igniting, establishing, and expanding the New Testament Church. I hope you were struck with awe as you watched Peter connect the prophecy from Joel 2, written about 400 years before he was born, to explain the tongues of fire over their heads. I hope you were stirred to wonder as you read about the churches pulling together to raise funds for a famine that was prophesied by Agabus (Acts 11:27-28), and I hope you let yourself wonder at how the Holy Spirit prophesied through an unnamed person to commission Barnabus and Saul and send them off as missionaries.

What about when Paul, filled with the Holy Spirit, told Elymas the magician, "You son of the devil, you enemy of all righteousness, full of all deceit and villainy, will you not stop making crooked the straight paths

---

*   Acts 1:11

of the Lord?"* Is this something you would see as a prophetic moment? I think we need to at least consider it, even though it is uncomfortable to our modern sensibilities. When we see the mission of the prophetic from Genesis to Revelation as calling us into alignment with the covenant, calibrating us with the eternal purposes of Christ, this could be understood as a prophetic moment.

One of my favorite prophetic moments in Acts is in chapter 27 during Paul's harrowing voyage. He is being taken from Jerusalem to Rome as a prisoner. Well into their exhausting journey, they find themselves camped in a cove waiting for the weather to improve. Paul says to them: "Men, I perceive that the voyage will certainly be with damage and great loss, not only of the cargo and the ship but also of our lives." The word perceive means to see, but it is more than that. It also means to sense, discern or feel in your gut. It is used by the woman at the well when she says to Jesus, "I perceive that you are a prophet."† It is that thing that we try to communicate when we see something that is beyond the obvious; we have a deeper hunch about something that is up ahead.

But they didn't listen. Of course, Paul is a prisoner. What does he know? They took the advice of the expert seamen, and a large group of their passengers all agreed.

Fast forward…they fought the winds for two solid weeks and were now convinced they were all going to die. They were exhausted on every possible level. Paul speaks up again.

"Men, you ought to have followed my advice and not to have set sail from Crete and incurred this damage and loss. Yet now I urge you to keep up your courage, for there will be no loss of life among you, but only of the ship. For this very night an angel of the God to whom I belong and whom I serve stood before me, saying, 'Do not be afraid, Paul; you must

---

* Acts 13:10 ESV
† John 4:19 ESV

stand before Caesar; and behold, God has granted you all those who are sailing with you.' Therefore, keep up your courage, men, for I believe God that it will turn out exactly as I have been told. But we must run aground on a certain island.'"*

In the first part of the story, we see Paul discerning disaster ahead. He had a sense that something was coming. He could feel the warning in the Spirit, and it was very accurate. The danger was real, but his warning was not heeded. In the second part of the story, we see God crashing into the situation, speaking, directing, and declaring His will and purpose.

This is so fascinating to me! Are both of these instances prophetic? Would the first story fall into more of a hunch? A discernment? A sense of what was to come, but not necessarily prophetically declaring the will of God? As you can see, the outcome of what Paul was initially discerning didn't actually happen. In the second story, we witness a profoundly prophetic moment as God unveils His plan for Paul to stand before Caesar, paving the way for the Gospel to go to Rome.

I think we should not be too quick to draw hard lines around these nuances. It's best to hold some of these things in mystery, even though we feel the tension. But I do love that we see an example of both of these realities in Scripture. Sometimes people can sense things to come, but it is important to remember that this is not to be taken as the express will of God. Is it still valuable information? Absolutely. But our response, our testing, and weighing, and our stewardship of these moments is different than when God speaks forth His direct will and instructions.

We could honestly spend months just studying through the prophetic stories in Acts. If we did, we would observe the characters in each story, wonder what they may have been thinking or feeling, watch the ways that heaven engages earth, and observe the mission and purpose of the Spirit

---

*   Acts 27:21-26

of Prophecy—and we would be struck with awe. But alas, this would be another study for another time.

For the rest of this chapter, we will lean in more deeply to a couple of important stories and watch the prophetic at work.

Ananias and Saul

Now there was a disciple at Damascus named Ananias; and the Lord said to him in a vision, "Ananias." And he said, "Here I am, Lord." And the Lord said to him, "Get up and go to the street called Straight, and inquire at the house of Judas for a man from Tarsus named Saul, for he is praying, and he has seen in a vision a man named Ananias come in and lay his hands on him, so that he might regain his sight." But Ananias answered, "Lord, I have heard from many about this man, how much harm he did to Your saints at Jerusalem; and here he has authority from the chief priests to bind all who call on Your name." But the Lord said to him, "Go, for he is a chosen instrument of Mine, to bear My name before the Gentiles and kings and the sons of Israel; for I will show him how much he must suffer for My name's sake." So Ananias departed and entered the house, and after laying his hands on him said, "Brother Saul, the Lord Jesus, who appeared to you on the road by which you were coming, has sent me so that you may regain your sight and be filled with the Holy Spirit." And immediately there fell from his eyes something like scales, and he regained his sight, and he got up and was baptized; and he took food and was strengthened (Acts 9:10-19).

We have very good friends who live in Damascus, Syria. I remember receiving a phone call from them in the middle of the Syrian war. They were asking for prayer, because the streets in their city were filled with people running and screaming to all who could hear, "ISIS is coming! ISIS is on their way!! Run! Hide! Take cover!!" In a mad panic, there were thousands of people crying, screaming, and grabbing as many things as they could carry as they ran for their lives. The tangible fear in the air was overwhelming. The Syrians had heard the stories of the brutality of ISIS, and it gave birth to terror in their souls.

It made me wonder if this fairly recent scene in Damascus was at all similar to when first-century followers of Jesus heard the news of Saul and his army heading their way. The evils these men had done in Jerusalem had caused fear to spread throughout the region. They had heard about Saul and his men hunting all who believed in Jesus, and they knew that he was going from house to house dragging men, women, and children to prison or stoning them to death. It was great persecution, indeed. And now they were on their way to Damascus to do the same.

Were the people running, screaming, and crying in the streets as my friends had experienced during the Syrian war? Were panic and hopelessness rising in the air as more and more people heard the news? Or were they hiding underground in silent hope that they could wait out the terror that was coming?

Historians believe that this part of the story occurred around AD 33-36. This is only a short time after the crucifixion and resurrection of Christ. The believers in Jerusalem, Damascus, and the surrounding region were new followers of The Way. They had only just begun to believe that Jesus was the Messiah for whom they had been waiting, and they were facing the ultimate test of faith.

This story is the first time Ananias appears on the scene. He's unknown to the reader until this dramatic moment, and we don't hear about him again after this event. This is his moment in the spotlight, and all the story tells us about him is that he's a disciple in Damascus, and he was a "devout man according to the law."* There is no reason to believe that Ananias held

---

*   Acts 22:12 ESV

any official position of leadership within the community, and there are no hints of his unique gifts or great accomplishments. As far as we can tell, he was just a normal Jesus follower, if there was such a thing in that day. We don't know how a Christian community developed in Damascus. It is possible that when disciples fled Jerusalem after the stoning of Stephen, they found themselves in Syria. Regardless, we are the privileged observers of Ananias' most defining moment.

Have you ever seen a little tugboat gently towing a massive ship out into the sea? It is quite a sight to behold. Somehow, this little tug boat is necessary in the launching of a disproportionate, extraordinary vessel. I can't help but envision Ananias like this. His brief moment on the stage seems to tow the great apostle into the deep. This mysterious man was chosen by God to ignite one of the most influential men in human history.

Let's go back and take another look at what God said to Ananias. His first words were, "Get up and go to the street called Straight, and inquire at the house of Judas for a man from Tarsus named Saul, for he is praying, and he has seen in a vision a man named Ananias come in and lay his hands on him, so that he might regain his sight."*

I am both fascinated by what God said to Ananias and what He didn't say. He told him where to go, but not what to say. He told him who would be there, but didn't tell him how he would be received. He told him to lay hands on a man, but should he pray for him? He knew that God had prepared the way for him by giving Saul a vision of Ananias, but Saul was currently blind. How would he know that this was the man?

I think we can presume that this felt life-threatening for Ananias. The risk was clear and obvious, and Ananias carefully voiced his concern. God's response was, "Go, for he is a chosen instrument of Mine, to bear My name before the Gentiles and kings and the sons of Israel; for I will

---

*   Acts 9:11 ESV

show him how much he must suffer for My name's sake.'"* There was no promise of survival for Ananias. No comforting words that he would come out of this alive. All he knew is that God had chosen this violent persecutor to be His instrument. How must this have felt for Ananias? Did this bother him? God did tell him that Saul would suffer for His name. Was this supposed to help?

Ananias is nothing less than heroic in my mind. As he walked out the ultimate test of faith, his level of obedience was stunning. I think the part of this passage that wrecks me the most is Ananias' first words to Saul when he walked in the door. "Brother Saul."† Brother? Why would he call this man 'brother'? Was this something that the Lord told him to say? It could be an appeal to their shared Jewish heritage, but I believe it is more than that.

It seems to me that once Ananias knew that this persecutor was going to become a follower of The Way, it was only natural that Ananias related to him as family. Yet they hadn't even met. I get overwhelmed when I ponder all that must have changed within Ananias' heart and mind as the Lord spoke to him. Somewhere on his own personal journey, the fear that Ananias had regarding this man had shifted completely into a compassionate "Welcome to the family." And this shift happened solely through the voice of God invading his very human heart.

I have experienced this more times than I can say. Not the persecution part, of course, but the transformation of my own heart within a single moment of God speaking. His voice transforms us as messengers as we carry His words.

I also notice the interaction between Ananias and God. Ananias didn't just "get a download." He had questions and concerns, and he wanted clarification. He discussed things with the Lord, and the Lord shared His

---

*   Acts 9:15 ESV
†   Acts 9:17

heart, purpose, and intentions with His messenger. It is relational to the core. It is all relational. God could have just done His work within Saul on His own, but He didn't. He didn't have to include Ananias in His plans with Saul, but He did. He didn't need to explain Himself to Ananias, but He did. He didn't need to transform Ananias' heart, but He did. For some reason, it was important to the Lord to move through a human vessel.

I wonder if it was because of what Saul was being saved into. He was not just being redeemed by the Lord and transformed into the most influential figure in Christian history, but he was being welcomed into the family of believers, the community of saints, the Body of Christ. I also find myself taking note of the fact that God did not promise Ananias that he would be safe or that this would go well for him. He didn't seem to answer the fear of Ananias. Instead, He explained the why of what he was being asked to do.

The other thing that strikes me is the symbolism. I hope you don't mind me pontificating a bit further here, as I do understand this is a stretch of the imagination. But I can't help but give a nod to the mystical metaphor of the prophetic opening the eyes of the apostolic and prophesying the road ahead. This interaction has the essence of the apostolic and prophetic working together to ignite and lay foundations. In so doing, the prophetic is opening the path for the Great Commission to unfold through this blind, broken Pharisee.

There is one more aspect of this story I would like to lean into, because I feel as if it can influence our thinking regarding some important nuances within the prophetic experience. It's interesting to pay attention to the recorded words God spoke to Ananias and compare them to the recorded words that Ananias spoke to Saul. They are not exact, word-for-word replicas. God spoke to Ananias:

And then He said these words in response to Ananias' question: "Go, for he is a chosen instrument of Mine, to bear My name before the Gentiles and kings and the sons of Israel; for I will show him how much he must suffer for My name's sake."*

What Ananias actually spoke to Saul was,

"Brother Saul, the Lord Jesus, who appeared to you on the road by which you were coming, has sent me so that you may regain your sight and be filled with the Holy Spirit."†

We don't know, of course, if there were many words that were left out of this printed retelling of the encounter, but the difference in wording is still a good thing to discuss. Luke's retelling of the story is most likely intentional. So what may he be saying through this particular phrasing? Ananias didn't say anything about what Saul was being called into. He didn't tell him the great things he was going to accomplish, or how much he was going to suffer for the Gospel. In fact, he didn't share anything that the Lord told him in response to his own questions. He only told Saul what God told him originally, and he didn't try to puff up Saul's ego by talking about the great things he was going to do. He didn't try to humble Saul with the promise of suffering. He was simply obedient to the request of the Lord.

Peter and Cornelius

Now we have the thrill of observing a momentous turn of events that was led entirely by visitations, encounters, and prophetic revelations. This is the kind of story that was told in hushed tones and secret rooms over and over again as the hearers would never tire of the profound, supernatural direction of God. These two visions of Peter and Cornelius opened the way for the explosive expansion of the Kingdom beyond the Jewish people.

---

*   Acts 9:15-16
†   Acts 9:17

Luke tells this dramatic story in both Acts 10 and again in Acts 11, then refers to the fruit of this experience in Acts 15:6–9. These passages reveal just how important these events are in the grand scope of the Gospel. They also give us a hint concerning the impact that these events had on the lives of the people who were involved. It is, of course, the initial fulfillment of Jesus' words in Matthew 8:11: "Many will come from the east and the west, and will take their places … in the kingdom of heaven."*

This series of prophetic encounters changed everything. Gentiles welcomed into the family of Yahweh? Adopted as brothers and sisters in the inheritance of heaven? To many Jews, it was too scandalous to even consider. It felt blasphemous and simply couldn't be God's will. To allow the impure into the fold was against everything they had ever believed. To welcome the stranger to sit amongst them, without circumcision, without ritual cleansing...how could this possibly be the plan of the Lord?

So, they told the story over and over again as proof that God's desire was for the Kingdom of heaven to spread from "Jerusalem and in all Judea, and Samaria, and as far as the remotest part of the earth."† In this story, we see the power that the prophetic has to alter the course of the Church, to change paradigms, and to upend our limited theological understanding.

Cornelius was a centurion in the Italian Regiment, a cohort of 600 Roman soldiers. He was a powerful, respected leader in a high position of authority. From the description in Acts 10 of Cornelius being devout and God-fearing, it can be inferred that he was not a full-fledged proselyte to Judaism. This meant that he had not been circumcised (Acts 11:3). And yet, he was respected by the Jews, which speaks volumes about his way of life. The time reference was three in the afternoon, and it most likely referred to the Jewish time of prayer (verse 3). The passage also noted that he was respected and was considered to have noble character. This respect was

---

*   Matthew 8:11 NIV
†   Acts 1:8 NIV

given for two primary reasons: he was generous, and he was a praying man.

Ponder this man with me for a moment. He is a strong, Italian, high-ranking soldier who was trying his best to pursue the God of a different people. Why would he do that? He was clearly very serious in his devotion. He had led his family, his servants, and at least some of his military aides into this devotion. What does this say about his character? What does this say about his passion, his personality, his leadership, and his humility?

Cornelius instantly sent three of his men to Joppa, some 33 miles south of Caesarea, to bring some man named Peter back with them—based solely on a vision! He sent them to walk 33 miles to go pick up a stranger at someone's house they didn't know. Did he have any doubt that they would find the house? Did he trust that there would actually be a man named Peter at that house? Would this man come willingly with his men, or would he resist and think they were crazy? The obedience in this story is beautiful.

Sit and put yourself inside this narrative, allowing yourself to feel what they may have felt. Ask the questions they may have been asking, and face the doubts and fears they may have been feeling. What compelled them to obedience? What pushed them past possible humiliation and embarrassment to pursue a vision? Have you ever been this obedient to something that felt crazy?

The vision of Peter on the rooftop becomes more astonishing the more you think about it (Acts 10:10–12). While hungry, Peter fell into a trance in which God gave him a vision of a sheet coming down to earth with all kinds of animals, reptiles, and birds. When God commanded Peter to eat of these animals, his response was, "By no means, Lord!" (verse 14).

Understandably so. The phrase "all kinds" means the inclusion of the whole animal kingdom, both on land and in the air, which we can assume included some animals that were unclean under Jewish law. If eaten, Peter would have become ritually defiled, unfit to come into God's presence in worship. Can you imagine the confusion Peter must have felt? Significantly, his refusal, "surely not," was the Greek word médamós[22], which is a more polite and subjective term than oudamós[23], which means "by no means" and is used only in Matthew 2:6. This is important to note, because it reveals the state of Peter's heart. It wasn't anger. It wasn't rebellion. It wasn't pride. It was genuine, humble confusion. We can't blame him. Why would God ask him to do something that was against everything He had said before? Why would God ask him to break the law, make himself impure, and break Jewish customs (Leviticus 11)? Was this a test?

"What God has cleansed, no longer consider unholy" (verse 15). Peter saw and heard this vision three times. I can't remember the last time someone told me something three times in a row. If they had, I would certainly know it must be extremely important. Three times isn't something you can ignore or brush off as some weird, undigested piece of food. Three times. It is important. Yet, Peter refused to eat the unclean foods three times. Why?

I can't help but flash back to Peter's denial of Christ. He denied knowing his Lord three times before the rooster crowed. And then, in his encounter with the risen Christ on the beach, Jesus asked him three times, "Do you love me?"* An exasperated Peter repeated his same answer three times. It does cause me to wonder if the repetition was a confirmation to Peter that it was truly the Lord speaking. Or maybe it was just God's way of being clear.

Either way, can you sit with me and imagine having this powerful, disruptive vision three times in a row? Imagine Peter's emotional state by the third time. Imagine his angst. Did he have fear? Was he worried about

---

* John 21:15-17

misunderstanding the Lord? Was he afraid that he wasn't understanding something that was important to grasp?

In marvelous timing and by the coordination of the sovereign God, the three messengers and Peter met. "While Peter was reflecting on the vision, the Spirit said to him, 'Behold, three men are looking for you. But get up, go downstairs and accompany them without misgivings, for I have sent them Myself.'"* Oh, the kindness of the Lord to interrupt Peter's processing and give him the next clue.

Notice how the Lord is working with Peter. Notice how the mission of the Lord is unfolding. What is God actually communicating to His sons, and what pieces of information is He withholding? This scene is like a grand chess match, and the players are left in their baffled state until the last minute. We understand the big-picture purpose of this event now, but can we climb inside of these men's lives and feel what they may have felt? What does this teach us about the ways of the Lord? What does this teach us about the ways of the prophetic? How does this compare to the prophetic function we see today?

By the time Peter and his guests finished lunch, it must have been too late to start back to Caesarea. The next day they began the almost two-day trip. Cornelius' men had left Caesarea after 3 p.m. one day and arrived at noon two days later, hence "four days ago" in verse 30. Peter took with him some of the brothers from Joppa. The two-by-two motif is common in the gospels and Acts. Christian workers often went out in groups of two. In this situation, it seems that at least six people accompanied Peter (11:12). So there would have been seven witnesses to attest to what would transpire.

Why did Peter bring so many with him? I can imagine how Peter may have felt the need for some extra backup! He was obeying the Lord into

---

*   Matthew 19-20

unchartered territory, pushing past all of his internal, instinctive, and well-taught boundaries of right and wrong. Oh, how I wish I could have heard Peter's thoughts as he was walking this long journey to a stranger's house, not knowing what was to come. Would he be mocked by his family? Would he be criticized, hated, or judged by his friends? He must have wondered if he was going a bit crazy, right? Yet, the super-charged spiritual atmosphere of these days must have also been exhilarating. He had seen the risen Christ, and there was no going back.

Cornelius was so confident that Peter would come, and he was so expectant about Peter's message, that he called together his relatives and close friends. This is full buy-in! Did he have any doubt that this was going to be life-changing? Was he at all wondering how this was going to unfold? He didn't fill the room with soldiers, ready to defend or protect. He filled the room with family and close friends. This speaks volumes!

When Peter arrived, Cornelius prostrated himself in worship before the apostle. The verb prosekynēsen means "he worshiped" and is here translated "in reverence."[24] Peter rejected this and urged Cornelius to stand up. "For," he said, "I am only a man." What does this tell us about Cornelius? He is a high-ranking soldier who is now on his face before a fisherman. As far as we know, he doesn't know anything about Peter, except that the Lord knows his name.

Peter was well aware of the consequences of fellowshipping with Gentiles in their homes. But by now, he must have learned the lesson of the vision, at least in part. As he opened his mouth to begin preaching the Gospel to this room full of hungry hearts, he said, "I most certainly understand God is not one to show partiality."* Of course, he understands this! He is one who denied Christ and who now carries the message of grace birthed out of his own brokenness.

---

* Acts 10:34

These words of Peter were revolutionary. They swept away the prejudice and indoctrination of generations of Judaism. The sovereign interruption of the Holy Spirit rapidly concluded Peter's message when He came on all those who heard and believed Peter's message about Jesus. The six circumcised believers were beside themselves at this evidence of the equality of Gentiles with Jewish believers.

It's important to note that the sign God used to validate the inclusion of Gentiles into the Kingdom was the outpouring of the Holy Spirit. This does cause me to pause and wonder if we would respond the same way in a similar situation today.

— CHAPTER 7 —

Stewardship of Power

At its most basic, the word power means having the ability to influence another person's behavior. It is the ability to do something, the capacity to master something, or the ability to dominate. It is inherent in being human. We have been given the power to steward the ground under our feet. We are given power by everyone who loves us. Even a gentle smile to the neighbor walking by our house is a form of power that is being stewarded because it has the ability to evoke emotion in another.

The point is that every human being is a force in this world. We have felt power coming toward us or through us. We have had a knee-jerk reaction to someone else's power, or we have wielded power ourselves—often unwittingly. Worse yet, we might have felt the sting of someone else's misuse of power. Power is a reality that we have all experienced, but it is one that we are often incognizant of until it raises its ugly head and tries to dominate or control.

Every form of abuse is an abuse of power. This much we are usually aware of. But we are often less aware of the power we steward over our loved ones every day. With a single glance, we can inflict shame or disgust, or we can wash someone in grace and love. This is power. When someone gives their heart permission to love and be loved, they make themselves vulnerable to others. Power exists in every relationship, whether we recognize it or not. It exists in leadership teams, worship teams, marriages, and friendships.

All of us have power. We submit to power when we obey a parent, teacher, coach, or counselor. Our pastors and leaders have the power to influence our lives through their guidance and teaching. At various times, we are the parent disciplining a child, the teacher handing out praise to children, the coach ordering the running of laps, etc. We have the power to hurt, reject, validate, or help. Power can be a personal resource that is used for the good of others and for the protection of the vulnerable. We can use our power to defend the oppressed, feed the poor, or help the wounded. Or we can use our power to dominate others, to strip them of their dignity, or to push them to the margins. Consciously or unconsciously, we experience power dynamics on a daily basis.

The stewardship of power is a profoundly important part of our discipleship process. Still, it's rarely directly addressed. We can all agree that humans have a very complicated relationship with power. In fact, I would say that there has been only One who has stewarded power perfectly, and that, of course, was Jesus. He held all the power of the universe within Him and demonstrated immense restraint. He regularly moved in miraculous power and set a constant example of the power wielded within leadership and influence. In fact, it was one of the most important things on his heart the night before he was crucified:

Then He poured water into the basin, and began to wash the disciples' feet and to wipe them with the towel with which He was girded. So He came to Simon Peter. He said to Him, "Lord, do You wash my feet?" Jesus answered and said to him, "What I do you do not realize now, but you will understand hereafter." Peter said to Him, "Never shall You wash my feet!" Jesus answered him, "If I do not wash you, you have no part with Me." Simon Peter said to Him, "Lord, then wash not only my feet, but also my hands and my head." Jesus said to him, "He who has bathed needs only to wash his feet, but is completely clean; and you are clean, but not all of you." For He knew the one who was betraying Him; for this reason He said, "Not all of you are clean." So when He had washed their feet, and taken His garments and reclined at the table again, He said to them, "Do you know what I have done to you? You call Me Teacher and Lord; and you are right, for so I am. If I then, the Lord and the Teacher, washed your feet, you also ought to wash one another's feet. For I gave you an example that you also should do as I did to you. Truly, truly, I say to you, a slave is not greater than his master, nor is one who is sent greater than the one who sent him."*

What a phenomenal teaching on the stewardship of power and authority! Jesus was their teacher, their Rabbi, their leader, and their Lord. He had the most power in the room, to put it mildly. His example was a direct message regarding how He used this authority, what He did with His power. It strikes me so deeply that this was one of our Lord's final teachings while on the earth.

The stewardship of power is a crucial conversation within the prophetic. Yet I have never heard teaching specifically about it. There are teachings on humility and submission. There are many teachings on learning how to harness spiritual power or how to stand in your authority. All these topics discuss elements of power, but they aren't usually getting to the root of this very important topic: we are called to be aware of the power we are wielding and to learn to steward it as Jesus did.

If we are going to discuss the maturing journey of a prophetic calling, gifting, or grace, we simply must discuss the stewardship of power. It's quite possible that the poor stewardship of power is the primary element that pulls the prophetic off base. I'm convinced that the lack of maturity in understanding power dynamics and having the character to steward

---

* John 13:5-15

power well is at the root of every prophetic blunder. Because of this, let's discuss the deep nuances of power. Let's become aware of the things we are normally unaware of until they cause wounding. Let's bring these power dynamics out of unspoken obscurity and into the light, making the intangible a bit more tangible.

Our first stop of exploration, as with everything, is within our own heart. Let's dig deep, my friend! Let's dig deep into self-reflection and not let the error of over-confident assumption be our downfall. None of us is immune to the temptation of power, so this is a muscle we must strengthen. Our aim is to become more aware of the power we are holding as we prophesy and grow in our ability to steward the many nuances of power according to the way of Jesus.

Have you been in a relationship in which you felt powerless? Was this an accurate and true reality, or just an emotional reaction to someone who was presuming too much power? Codependency is actually rooted in an emotional construct of powerlessness. Many forms of depression are rooted in a victim mindset, also known as a false sense of powerlessness. Various personalities will instinctively grasp for power, while other personalities will instinctively feel powerless and victimized by the world around them.

Can we take a moment and do some soul-searching? Which way would you lean? There are ditches on every side of this equation, and there's always more to learn. Think of all the ways in which you acted with power and influence over the last couple of days. What did that look like? For example, did you encourage someone you loved today? Did that influence them with the power of your love? Did you speak to a customer service person today? Did you offer them kindness or irritation? (Both responses are moments of wielding power). Did you instruct your child or obey your boss?

Were you aware of your stewardship of power in those moments, or did you know that you had a choice in how you used that power? Can you think of an example when you stewarded power selflessly? Can you think of another time when you stewarded power selfishly? What changed in each circumstance to compel your choices? If you felt powerless in a situation, can you pause and see if that is actually true? Or maybe it was just an emotional belief system.

Studies conducted by the Baylor University School of Social Work discovered that many Christians do not understand that power is a characteristic of human relationships.[25] Nor do they discuss the responsibilities and privileges that come with that power. Misunderstanding or ignoring the power structures in our lives creates the vulnerability of abuse. Our response to the most helpless human beings exposes who we are. The way we wield power—how we respond to those who have less power than ourselves, how we deal with frustration, how we decide to lead others, how we accomplish tasks, etc.—-will inevitably expose our character. Power will expose character every single time.

Within the Christian world, this includes the added element of spiritual power. We need to pause and carefully consider the power and influence that comes with spiritual gifts. These gifts are a manifestation of supernatural power. To experience the power of the Holy Spirit moving through us to heal a human body, or to speak revelation from heaven that no one should know, or to see miracles happen before our eyes is an overwhelming experience. If we are going to walk in this kind of power well, we must lean into a deeper understanding of power and its effect on us and others.

Our best example of beautiful stewardship of power is Christ Himself. So let's lean into the person of Jesus and observe.

Jesus and Power

If we spend any time contemplating God as He was experienced by Ezekiel during his vision (Ezekiel 1-3), or through John's experience in Revelation 4, or Isaiah's dramatic throne-room encounter (Isaiah 6), we will undoubtedly be brought to our knees. This kind of holiness shreds the human heart to pieces. The level of glory these men witnessed is so overwhelming that they felt death was imminent. It gives new meaning to the word awe. Isaiah's sin was so clear and vivid in the unfettered presence of our Creator that he screamed, "Woe is me!" He was utterly convinced that he was seeing something that was impossible for human eyes to see and still live.

If we take a slow walk through the inauguration of the first temple in 2 Chronicles 7 and allow our hearts to imagine the experience of such power and glory filling a man-made dwelling, how does this influence our view of the incarnation of Christ? This God from Revelation 4, this power from Ezekiel's vision, this same holiness and glory we see in Isaiah's encounter was inside of this man Jesus as He walked the earth. How can we even begin to process all that this implies? It will take all of human history to barely scratch the surface of such a truth. In the incarnation, the majesty, wholeness, purity, and love of the Trinity became clothed with fearful, ashamed, and muddied humanity. The glory of God became one with broken and fallen humanity. It is unfathomable, yet it is at the core of our Christian faith.

In your relationships with one another, have the same mindset as Christ Jesus:

Who, being in very nature God, did not consider equality with God something to be used to his own advantage; rather, he made himself nothing by taking the very nature of a servant, being made in human

likeness. And being found in appearance as a man, he humbled
himself by becoming obedient to death —even death on a cross!*

The One who holds the universe in the span of His hand was fully
and completely God in the womb of a fourteen-year-old girl. "Jesus said
to them, 'Truly, truly I say to you, before Abraham was born, I am.'"† He
walked this earth as the "I AM." This should take our breath away. The
same God we read about in Isaiah 6—the immensity of His power, the
magnitude of His Glory, the Unfathomable One Himself—was incarnated
into this world in human flesh. This same God that John saw in Revelation
4 entered into our existence.

He didn't cease being God. He didn't lay down His deity in order to
become human. He remained fully God, and He clothed Himself with
humanity. This is the great mystery and miracle of the incarnation! Jesus
was fully God and fully human. In becoming human, He was never
anything less than fully God. Yet, He never relied on His deity; He never
pulled out all the stops and used His immense power as God while He
walked on the earth. This Philippians 2 passage is so shocking, and it has
many implications.

We want desperately to believe that He manifested the fullness of His
deity when He raised the dead, healed broken bodies, and moved in miraculous power. But that is not true. He walked as a human, fully filled with
the Holy Spirit, just as we are today. It is vital that we understand this, or
we will not be able to embrace the fullness of His redemption and His
example for humanity. He walked the path that all of His followers were
going to walk: fully human and fully filled with the Holy Spirit.

Do you see the difference here? If He had used the full power of His
deity, He would not have paved the way for a new humanity. He "did

---

*   Philippians 2:5-8 NIV
†   John 8:58

not consider equality with God something to be used to his own advantage."* Jesus did not leave His deity behind, but He humbled Himself by becoming obedient to the limitations of humanity. He had a choice to make every day that He walked this earth. His choice was either to be obedient to the limitations of humanity or to rely upon His deity, pulling out His God-card.

What wrecks me, among many things in this passage, is the humility of His restraint. Just think of all the moments He may have been tempted to show His true power! Did He have moments where He wanted to smite someone? Put them in their place? Think of all the times He was judged, misunderstood, gossiped about, and slandered publicly. Just think of the betrayal of his friend. Or what about the arrogance of the Pharisees? Oh, what I would have wanted to do to put them in their place if I had held that kind of power within me! Never did He say, "I don't deserve that," or assert His rights. He felt the sting of rejection and scorn from the very ones He was going to die to save.

> *Who has measured the waters in the hollow of his hand*
> *and marked off the heavens with a span,*
> *enclosed the dust of the earth in a measure*
> *and weighed the mountains in scales*
> *and the hills in a balance?*
> *Who has measured the Spirit of the LORD,*
> *or what man shows him his counsel?*
> *Whom did he consult,*
> *and who made him understand?*
> *Who taught him the path of justice,*
> *and taught him knowledge,*
> *and showed him the way of understanding?†*

---

*   Philippians 2:6 NIV
†   Isaiah 40:12-14 ESV

This Jesus instructed us to turn the other cheek. This Jesus instructed leaders to wash the feet of those they are in charge of. This Jesus said if they demand your coat, give them your shirt, too (Luke 6:29). The level of love and humility in our Jesus is absolutely overwhelming.

"Have the same mindset as Christ Jesus." Oh goodness gracious...do we need to say more? We are followers of this Jesus, speaking His words out of our mouths. And He has shown us how He wants us to handle this power—with great humility, great restraint, great love, great authority, great meekness, and great wisdom. I could go on and on. This is why the discussion of prophetic maturity is one and the same with the discussion of our discipleship into the Lordship of Christ Jesus.

As our character matures, so does our gift. As our humility deepens, so does our gift. As our awe of our God overtakes us, worship becomes the only natural response. As we mature, we will be formed into His likeness, reflecting His image into the earth. This is the calling of all followers, so how much more would it be the calling for the prophets? Can we walk with His power and His humility? Not turning away one for the other, but in full surrender, learning to allow the Holy Spirit to have full access to our heart, mind, and soul, molding our hearts into sons and daughters who are trustworthy with the power He has given us.

David and Power

In 1 Samuel 17, David confronts Goliath. We know the story of this young boy who goes up against the mighty Goliath with a slingshot and five smooth stones. Was David considered a powerful person in society at this point in his life? Or a powerful person physically? Was he a powerful warrior with his own abilities or talents in the arena of battle? The answer, of course, is no. Children were the smallest and least powerful people in David's time (and in most societies around the world today).

The picture of the socially powerless against the perceived powerful is clearly represented in this story. At this moment, David is disadvantaged in every way but one: his need. I know it sounds a bit strange to acknowledge need as power, but in our upside-down Kingdom, it is most certainly true. In his desperate need, he recognizes his powerlessness, and instead of panicking, running, screaming, or becoming angry at his own smallness, he embraces complete reliance upon the Lord alone. He surrenders the battle before him into the hands of God and leans upon his Maker completely.

As David leans into his weakness (rather than pushing against it), he experiences a kind of oneness with God. David embraces his need rather than judging it as a problem. He surrenders to his weakness so fully that His powerlessness becomes the very thing that makes him powerful. This is what Paul is talking about when he says things like, "That is why, for Christ's sake, I delight in weaknesses, in insults, in hardships, in persecutions, in difficulties. For when I am weak, then I am strong."* His powerlessness is the very thing that gives him great power. This is the essence of being poor in spirit. The more we accept our need and lean into our weakness, the more deeply surrendered we are to His presence, His strength, His power, and His love. Our powerlessness draws us into utter dependence.

Oh, how we push against weakness! Our culture exalts strength and power everywhere, and much of this mindset has leaked into our churches. We elevate those who can preach powerfully. We exalt the influencers, the politically powerful, and the famous. How has this affected our view of the Kingdom? I think its effects are deeply rooted and are cultivating a silent disdain for weakness. Many of us feel this disdain most acutely when we feel weakness within our own soul. When we are suddenly awakened

---

*   2 Corinthians 12:10 ESV

to our own humanity, we often struggle with self-criticism or even self hatred.

Many of us see weakness as a problem that needs to be fixed rather than a gift that we are invited to embrace. We see strength and weakness as contradictory, so we cannot see that true strength is found within our weakness. This is what young David instinctively knew as he prepared to face Goliath, and this is what the apostle Paul knew after his encounter on the Damascus Road. Paul delighted in his weaknesses, because he had discovered the beauty of how the two were the meeting place of the presence and power of God. When was the last time you didn't bemoan your weakness but boasted in it? Did you notice that the power of Christ rested upon you, as Paul wrote in 2 Corinthians 12:9?

In the truest sense of our humanity, we are in desperate need. We rely on grace to take our next breath. We can't force our own heart to beat. We need shelter from the elements of the world around us, and we require food to eat and water to drink in order to remain alive. We cannot truly live without the love of others, without tender touch, and without care from loved ones. We are indeed dependent. But many of us walk around this world acting as if we are in need of nothing, in denial of the innate weakness of our humanity.

God regularly invites us into a full embrace of this weakness, because that is where we will truly find Him. He is the giver and sustainer of our life and the lover of our souls. The core of our discipleship should always lead us back to an awareness of our need, into poverty of spirit, and teach us to rest in our complete dependence upon the Lord. The grasping for power we see in this world, and in the Church, is running in the opposite direction of this invitation into weakness. In the exact moments when we experience the power of the Holy Spirit moving through us, only the awareness of our own dependence leads us to safety. Finding the treasure is discovering that we can surrender fully to His power in our mind, our spirit, and our body while simultaneously remembering that it is not ours to grab hold of. It is here, in the weakness of our humanity, that we become conduits for His power while remaining firmly in His grasp.

"Blessed are the poor in spirit, for theirs is the kingdom of heaven."* We will be happiest when we admit that we have need because it gives us a sense of absolute dependence upon God. It is then that we will truly know who we are and who God is, and we will find rest in this knowing. And then the Kingdom will rest on us, for ours is the Kingdom.

If we were sitting across the table from each other right now, I would ask you about your emotional response to weakness, and then I would ask you about your emotional response to power. Do you avoid being seen as weak at all costs? Do you strive to be seen as powerful in your community? Do you grasp for power, or do you run away from it? Do you respect people of great power? Do you critically judge people you see as weak? Do you long to be powerful? Are you afraid of being powerful? How do you relate to the innate weakness you feel within yourself? Have you been wounded by someone else's abuse of power? How do you feel when the Holy Spirit speaks in and through you? Will you ponder this with me and do some self-reflection?

Our journey as prophetically gifted people is greatly influenced by our relationship to various forms of power, and this is directly related to our response to weakness. Learning to walk in the power of the prophetic is no small thing. Growing in our ability to handle the attention, as well as the slander, with the same heart-stance of humility and need defines the path on which we walk.

Our human desire for power is never to be underestimated. Our compulsive desire for control is never to be swept under the rug. Our fleshly desire for influence, ascendency, and dominion should never be

---

*   Matthew 5:3 ESV

ignored. If you don't know that you hold a sword in your hands, you will wound someone. And the one who becomes wounded may be you. Learning how to steward power is not an option. If we ignore it, we will abuse it. It has been given to us for a reason. Let's learn what that reason is. Authority and power have been given to us to accomplish something. Let's learn what we are to accomplish.[26]

> Power without love is reckless and abusive, and love without power
> is sentimental and anemic. Power at its best is love implementing the
> demands of justice, and justice at its best is power correcting every-
> thing that stands against love. - Martin Luther King Jr.[27]

— CHAPTER 8 —

Testing and Weighing

If God is speaking, it matters. It really matters. In many charismatic circles, we have made intentional efforts to normalize the voice of God, and I understand why. We desperately wanted everyone to hear His voice for themselves, which is a worthy mission. But along the way, many of us didn't take the time to clarify the difference between hearing God's voice, discernment, and the prophetic. It was all clumped together under the word "prophetic," so everything became prophetic. It was as if the word "prophetic" became synonymous with the activity of the Holy Spirit.

We intentionally and methodically worked to demystify the prophetic to make it accessible for all, which is right and good—if the prophetic simply means to hear God's voice. But it doesn't. Plus, we have created safe atmospheres for people to experiment and make many mistakes, which is wonderful on so many levels. Yet, some of the harmful fruit that has come out of this approach is:

1) We haven't taught people the difference between putting up their spiritual antenna and truly hearing God's voice. There is a massive difference between these two things. In many places, we have blurred these lines so profoundly that people now believe that anything they feel/sense/see/hear is probably God speaking. This isn't so.

2) We can normalize the prophetic so much and created such safe places for mistakes that it's often treated way too casually. We have lost the tremble, the awe, the holy knee-wobble that should come with the voice of God breaking into our lives. In this offhanded, improvisational style of teaching people to hear God's voice, we have created a culture that can be borderline on the ear-tickling circus shows Scripture warns us of. It can also nurture a response to His voice that permits obedience to be optional. Combine that with the reality that in many circles there is literally zero testing and weighing or responsible follow-up concerning what is being prophesied, you have a mess on your hands.

If God is speaking, then it matters. It really matters. If someone is claiming that it is God speaking and it is not actually Him, that matters, too. It really matters. We don't want to become careless with the voice of God. If He is speaking, then we need to be responding. I think the verses in the Bible that command us to weigh the prophetic carefully are central for the healthy empowerment of this calling. That means our church leaders, our prophets, and, well, the whole Body of Christ, need to become more adept in testing and weighing in order to honor His voice in the way He deserves.

Every prophetic moment involves both a communicator and a receiver. Whether the Lord is moving through an individual to communicate with one person or He is communicating with thousands of people, there is always both the message carrier and the recipient(s). In order for the prophetic to grow into maturity, both sides of this equation must be nurtured. Picture a handshake. Someone puts his hand out for a handshake and the other party grabs his hand and shakes it in response. The action isn't complete until both hands meet. The same is true with the prophetic—the message of the Lord must leave one person and enter into the hands of another. The two must meet in order for it to be complete.

Within my current tradition, nearly all of the emphasis is on the prophetic word being given. We teach people how to prophesy, help them to hear the voice of God, and instruct them on the anointing of the Holy Spirit, but very little time is spent on equipping the broader Body of Christ to be healthy receivers. In fact, most of the prophetic horror stories I have heard over the years include just as many mistakes from the receiver as the prophet.

In reality, they both have equal parts to play. They are equally responsible. As both hands meet for the handshake, there needs to be an acknowledgment of equal authority to pursue a proper understanding of what the Lord is communicating. Just listen to the following verses. Each of these commands speaks directly to the recipient with instruction on how to respond to prophecy:

"Two or three prophets should speak, and the others should weigh carefully what is said."*

"Do not quench the Spirit; do not despise prophetic utterances. But examine everything carefully; hold fast to that which is good; abstain from every form of evil."†

"Beloved, do not believe every spirit, but test the spirits to see whether they are from God, because many false prophets have gone out into the world."‡

Do you remember when we studied the difference between Old Testament and New Testament prophetic function? One of the biggest differences is that the prophets in the New Testament are not given the same amount of authority as they are in the Old Testament. One of the main reasons we know this is because of the instruction that we are to test and weigh prophetic words, which calls the prophet into submission. This

---

*   1 Corinthians 14:29 NIV
†   1 Thessalonians 5:19-22
‡   1 John 4:1

is truly a dramatic shift of the level of authority from what the prophet was carrying in the Old Testament!

On this side of Pentecost, everyone can hear the voice of God in a new way. So we're prophesying to people who also hear His voice and who are urged to weigh revelation for themselves. This means that there is an equalizing of the stewardship of the prophetic. In the Old Testament, the prophets prophesied and, in general, people were expected to listen and obey. If they did not, they would be considered in rebellion to His will. In the New Testament, the prophetic is brought into community, humility, and partnership.

It is important to take note that each of Paul's letters was written to the churches. He was speaking to communities of people who were in a relationship with him and with each other. The verses above point to the fact that this gift was primarily to function within community. This means that the whole community needs to learn how to relate to this gift, because they all have a part to play. I am convinced that the prophetic won't rise up into maturity and carry the power it's intended for until the Body of Christ grows in its ability to discern, test, and weigh—together.

Learning to do the work of testing and weighing is fundamental. We all long to hear God's voice. We deeply long to receive His words, His insight, His direction, His warning, His comfort, and His love. Every time there is a possibility He is speaking, we want to draw close to listen. As we seek to find His voice together, we must also test and weigh what we are hearing. In so doing, we will learn to trust in His voice in greater measure and take what we are hearing to heart. Isn't that the goal?

Our heart stance as we test and weigh is very important. We should not be standing in a place of arrogance judging another person's gift or critiquing someone's ability to get it right. We should not be standing in a place of over-confidence in which we think that we know more than the person who is prophesying. The prophet does not sit under our scrutiny.

Instead, we should remain in a place of humility and hunger, searching for the voice of our Creator—our beloved, cherished, and honored King. That is what matters.

I am also aware that the same measure of mercy and kindness I give to others is what I can expect to be given back to me. And the Lord knows how much mercy and kindness I need! Remember that the person sharing this word is human. They're just like us. We're all simply doing our best to hear from heaven. And most of the time, it takes a great amount of courage for someone to share what they've heard. Let's honor their courage, presume the best of everyone's heart, and sort things out with grace and love.

Another important aspect of testing and weighing the prophetic that is rarely mentioned is the need for self-awareness. We must pay attention to what is happening in our own mind and emotions as we hear/read/listen to a prophetic word. We are to weigh by the Spirit, not by our human instincts working independently of God's divine wisdom. Prophetic words are not subject to our mind, our opinions, or our pet doctrines. They are subject to the Lordship of Christ, to Scripture, and to the Spirit of Truth.

So when I hear a word, I must search my own heart first. Are my emotions reacting as I hear a prophetic word? If I find myself reacting in fear to a prophetic word, I cannot automatically say that the prophecy must be wrong. My emotional reactions cannot be confused with discernment. If I find myself reacting to a prophetic word in anger, pride, or anxiety, then I must separate out my reactions, triggers, and emotional responses and not let them interfere with discerning and receiving what the Lord is (or may be) speaking. Learning to separate my complex emotions from true discernment is a crucial part of growing in this gift.

Finally, the most important thing we need to do is discern the voice of the Holy Spirit in and through the words shared. This isn't something that is learned with a set of criteria for us to think through. No matter who is speaking, no matter what is happening, our hearts need to be longing to hear Him at all times. Then our heart will begin to lead the way. Our heart and the Holy Spirit will pull us toward His voice. We will begin to sense His movement within the words spoken. We will learn to feel His voice when He's speaking, regardless of who He is speaking through.

He is inviting us to live our lives seeking His voice through every possible avenue, and we eagerly do so when we're in love. The primary exercise is not simply to be able to test and weigh the prophetic. Our first call is to love His voice with our whole being. As we learn to be driven by love, we will let go of our unfounded certainties, our opinions, and our selfish desires and simply seek to know Him, to follow Him, and to hear Him.

When we first listen to a prophetic word, we should acknowledge that there are several things happening simultaneously. Within the message given, there is often a mixture of personal opinion, spirit, revelation, our understanding of things, our emotional response, etc. The complexity of the moment can sometimes make it a bit daunting to process. My common response, at least emotionally, is to "put it on the table" and process it more thoroughly later.

Sometimes I say that out loud, especially if I'm not sure the word has hit me well. I'll just gently ask the person who has prophesied (if it's to me, personally), "Can I just put that on the table for now to give me time to pray it through?" Most often though, I just internally picture myself putting it on a table in front of me. It helps create a pause in between the deepest part of my soul and the words that were just shared. This pause is incredibly important, because it honors the testing and weighing mandate. It's not the same as a wall of self-protection. It's not the same as having an unteachable heart or being closed to the voice of God. It's actually a very powerful stance that helps me take my responsibility seriously.

When I sit down to pray through that word, it often feels as if I am staring at a pile of laundry. I first need to put things in their right piles. Whites in one pile, colors in another, delicates in another. Sorting things a little first helps cultivate more clarity. With every prophetic word, we begin with at least three "piles."

Revelation - The raw data. What exactly did they see/hear/sense/feel from the Lord?

This is important for (hopefully) obvious reasons, but it is not always easy to pinpoint. Most of us who are prophetically gifted jumble a bunch of things together when we're sharing. There is nothing wrong with this, of course. But it's helpful to look for the original point of revelation and separate it from the rest of the communication. For instance, if someone says, "I saw this picture and I think the Lord was speaking," I put the picture in a separate category from the person's thoughts about the picture. If I am having a challenging time discerning the original message, I will often ask them specifically, "Can you tell me just the raw data of what you feel the Lord showed you?"

Interpretation - How did the receiver interpret the original revelation? What filters or framework did the receiver have that may have slanted the meaning of the word?

This is an important part of the word to consider because the person who received the message from the Lord would very likely have a sense of what He was intending to communicate, but it's helpful to put it in a separate pile. It does need to be considered and weighed separately because this is where our filters come into play.

Every one of us has filters. Prophets live within a culture that has a certain language, mindset, and values. They have passions and belief systems, wounds and brokenness. They have a history that has built an emotional construct, and they have hopes and dreams as well as pains and losses rolling around inside of them. We all do. These life experiences have the tendency to create filters through which everyone sees. So when the Lord shares something with any one of us, our interpretation of that word will nearly always be influenced by our filters. And that is okay. But it's something that needs to be weighed separately.

Application - What did the person think was to be done in response to this word? How did he or she apply it? Is the receiver's application accurate and biblical? What is his or her filter and framework for thinking through the application?

This is where things can get a bit sticky. Many prophetically gifted people feel as if they know how the receiver should apply the words spoken. I would suggest, however, that this may not always be so. Yes, there were times in Scripture where the one who was prophesying also had an understanding of what people were to do in response, such as Paul in Acts 27 on the ship headed for Rome. An angel of the Lord spoke to him and gave clear instructions for the men on the ship.

After they had gone a long time without food, Paul stood up before them and said: "Men, you should have taken my advice not to sail from Crete; then you would have spared yourselves this damage and loss. But now I urge you to keep up your courage because not one of you will be lost; only the ship will be destroyed. Last night an angel of the God to whom I belong and whom I serve stood beside me and said, 'Do not be afraid, Paul. You must stand trial before Caesar; and God has graciously given you the lives of all who sail with you.' So keep up your courage, men, for I have faith in God that it will happen just as he told me. Nevertheless, we must run aground on some island."[*]

In contrast, we see this moment in Acts when Agabus prophesies to Paul:

---

[*]   Acts 27:21-26 NIV

Coming over to us, he took Paul's belt, tied his own hands and feet with it and said, "The Holy Spirit says, 'In this way the Jewish leaders in Jerusalem will bind the owner of this belt and will hand him over to the Gentiles.'"*

Then the people tried to apply this prophecy and told Paul that he wasn't supposed to go to Rome. But Paul felt God had told him to go.

When we heard this, we and the people there pleaded with Paul not to go up to Jerusalem. Then Paul answered, "Why are you weeping and breaking my heart? I am ready not only to be bound, but also to die in Jerusalem for the name of the Lord Jesus." When he would not be dissuaded, we gave up and said, "The Lord's will be done."†

I love that this example is in the Bible! It is a beautiful story of how we can experience a prophetic moment, try to apply it, but have our application be off base. It is helpful to know that the application of prophecies should be weighed separately.

How Do We Weigh?

In order to test or measure anything, we need to know what we're measuring it up against. We don't want to hold it up in thin air and try to figure it out in obscurity. We need a measuring stick. We need something to hold it up against to see if it aligns with what we know is true. So after we sort the laundry a bit, we can take each pile and weigh it out separately.

---

*   Acts 21:11 NIV

†   Acts 21:12-14 NIV

The Measuring Stick

There is one ultimate test and three subtests. The ultimate test is truly the person of Jesus, by which everything in our faith is defined. The subtests break things down into three categories of consideration, and those categories are the Gospel, love, and community.

The Test of Jesus

The number one test is, of course, the person of Jesus. Can we see Jesus? Can we sense His voice? Can we feel His DNA? Is He glorified? Is this leading me toward Jesus or not? Can I hear, see, taste, and discern the character of Christ, the mission of Christ, and the purposes of Christ through this prophetic moment? I know this seems like it should be obvious, but it's often missed. He is the prophetic. He is the Word made flesh. "And I fell at his feet to worship him. But he said to me, 'See that you do not do that! I am your fellow servant, and of your brethren who have the testimony of Jesus. Worship God! For the testimony of Jesus is the spirit of prophecy.'"*

The Subsequent Tests

The Subsequent Three Tests (as presented by theologian James Dunn): The test of the Gospel (1 Corinthians 12:3), the test of love (1 Corinthians 13) and the test of community (1 Corinthians 12-14).[28]

---

* Revelation 19:10 NKJV

The Gospel

Does this prophecy align with the Gospel? Does it point to the Gospel, uphold the Gospel, and stand in agreement with the whole Gospel message? Does this prophecy "preach" the Gospel in its essence? Does it carry the Spirit, the purpose, and the heart of the Gospel?

Love

Does this prophecy carry love in its essence? Does it uphold the call and the intent of love, and does it point to the eternal love of God? Does this prophecy draw attention to Love Himself?

Community

Is this prophecy submitted to community? How does it hold up within the context of community? Can it withstand the spotlight of many eyes and ears who know and love you?

Further Considerations Scripture

You may be wondering why I waited until now to mention the importance of prophecy aligning with Scripture. I absolutely believe this is vital! But I also think it's more complex than we make it out to be. It doesn't take much effort to look across human history and see how people have used Scripture verses to justify unthinkable evils in the world. How we relate to Scripture matters. Finding one passage in the Bible, isolating it, removing it from its context and using it to justify a single prophetic word is not synonymous with weighing prophecy (or anything else) according to Scripture. We need to weigh the prophetic with the whole of Scripture, meaning that all prophetic utterances should align with a robust, healthy theology built upon the entire God story. Take, for instance, the vision

Peter had on the rooftop in Acts 10. We know now that this entire story between Peter and Cornelius fully lines up with Scripture, but Peter didn't realize this at the time. We need to have a few theologians we can lean on for further evaluation in times like these. I know this sounds intimidating because, let's be honest, most of us lack in our theological training. But this is one of the primary things I believe needs to change, especially amongst prophetically gifted and called individuals.

Encouragement

"But the one who prophesies speaks to people for edification, exhortation, and consolation."* I have heard messages that teach that all prophecies must be one of these three things. But this verse was never meant to be the final, defining law or box within which all prophecies are to fit. This verse is instructive but not exhaustive. Doing a thorough study of each of these words (edification, exhortation, and consolation) offers a very broad scope of concepts.

Would the book of Revelation fit within one of these three criteria? It all depends on how you define each of these terms. It all feels so relative, and therein lies the challenge. Our culture views encouragement much differently than the Middle East or Asia does. The Western way of life holds comfort in high esteem, and we have likely read this Scripture through our cultural lens, then created an entire theology around it. I can't tell you how often I've heard people say things like, "If it feels negative or discouraging, then throw it away." This rationale is unbiblical and based on emotional reasoning, which is a cognitive distortion.

Can we first address our own emotional health in these moments instead of tossing out the possibility that the Lord is speaking? This, of course, is not a license to be harsh, rude, or to wound people carelessly

---

*   1 Corinthians 14:3

while claiming to hear His voice. God is love. We are to be moved by love, empowered by love, and captured by love with every word shared. But to equate love with comfort is a mistake.

Accuracy

We do not test and weigh according to accuracy alone.

If we tested and weighed according to accuracy, Jonah should have been stoned as a false prophet (Jonah 3:4). He said that in forty days Nineveh would be destroyed. We, however, know that it wasn't. Was he a false prophet? No. The people repented, and God changed His mind. Consider the following passage.

It happened that as we were going to the place of prayer, a slave woman who had a spirit of divination met us, who was bringing great profit to her masters by fortune-telling. She followed Paul and us and cried out repeatedly, saying, "These men are bond-servants of the Most High God, who are proclaiming to you a way of salvation." Now she continued doing this for many days. But Paul was greatly annoyed, and he turned and said to the spirit, "I command you in the name of Jesus Christ to come out of her!" And it came out at the very moment (Acts 16:16-18).

The woman with a spirit of divination could have appeared to have been prophesying accurately about the apostles' call and the message they were bringing, and yet she was doing so from a wrong spirit. There is a possibility that she was prophesying that Paul and Silas were servants of "the Most High God," but meant Theos Hypsistos or Zeus. This may have been what the residents of Philippi would have understood from her words.

Either way, Paul knew this was not from the Holy Spirit. He tolerated her declarations for several days, maybe because she wasn't speaking anything that would hinder the Gospel from coming forth, but it was still causing irritation to his spirit. Eventually, when he could bear it no longer, Paul cast it out.

Being able to train your senses to discern when the Holy Spirit is speaking—versus when the words are someone's interpretation/opinion/influence—is both a gift of the Spirit and a muscle that can be strengthened (Hebrews 5:14). Most of our discernment happens in deep places within our heart and spirit. In most cases, weighing a prophecy isn't a mental exercise. It takes time to sit in deep places and sense the movement of the Holy Spirit as you search for the voice of the Lord. Overall, make sure that the prophetic word draws your attention to the Lord Jesus (Revelation 19:10).

The Spirit

We are to test and weigh the spirit that is behind the prophetic word.

"Beloved, do not believe every spirit, but test the spirits to see whether they are from God, for many false prophets have gone out into the world."* When John the Baptist was in his mother's womb and she came into the presence of Jesus, he leaped. I love this because it gives me a physical picture of what it feels like spiritually. When Jesus is speaking, the indwelt Holy Spirit seems to leap inside of me. Much like John in his mother's womb, in the presence of Christ, our "baby" leaps. Our spirit testifies that the Holy Spirit of God is present and that Jesus Christ is being glorified in that moment.

"The Spirit Himself testifies with our spirit that we are children of God."† There have been times when I have been given an accurate prophetic word, but the spirit behind it felt questionable. This is difficult to steward because we (especially in the West) feel highly uncomfortable with intangible realities. We want to look at something concrete in order

---

*   1 John 4:1 ESV
†   Romans 8:16

to agree or disagree with facts. But the Lord is calling us to lean into a true and deep relationship with the Holy Spirit so that He can lead us.

We must acknowledge that we believe in a very real spiritual dimension, as well as complex emotional realities both internally and externally, and all that includes many intangibles. The negative feelings we're experiencing may come from an unhealthy place within ourselves, a defensive reaction, or an emotional trigger. In this case, we need to own our personal emotional reactions and learn to separate them from the prophetic word. We may feel that something isn't right because of the way the person is sharing, because there's a motive behind the words that is unholy, or because the words themselves are simply not from the Lord. In any case, it is important that we pay attention to our gut instincts. We should hold such prophetic words at a distance until they can be looked at more deeply and discerned more thoroughly.

Character

We are to weigh the character of Christ in the life of the person giving the word.

Character matters. I'm not sure how we have gotten to the place in our Christian culture where somehow bad character is excused for the sake of gifting. This begs the question of how we define spiritual maturity. Is maturity in gifting synonymous with increased power and accuracy in gifting? Does maturity in the prophetic mean increased supernatural activity, like angelic encounters, gold dust, feathers falling out of nowhere, or impressive words of knowledge? Although these experiences are truly amazing, the answer must be a resounding no. Experiential spirituality in and of itself cannot be allowed to define maturity. Many people are incredibly gifted and yet very immature. Many people are anointed with power yet dreadfully lack character. The gifts and callings of God are without apology (Romans 11:29). They do not measure worth and value. Power does not indicate intimacy, and the supernatural is not a sign of internal oneness with the Holy Spirit. Scripture is clear on this.

We've all witnessed how some truly anointed and powerful evangelists, healers, and prophets were walking in great sin while moving in significant power. It is indeed possible for unhealthy and immature people to learn supernatural tricks and keys while neglecting their personal, intimate journey with Jesus. We can quite easily find ourselves learning how to move in the anointing of the Kingdom without being in submission or walking in union with the King Himself.

If we're not to seek growth in the supernatural per se, what do we pursue? How do we grow in our understanding of the true prophetic calling?

"In everything set them an example by doing what is good. In your teaching show integrity, seriousness and soundness of speech that cannot be condemned, so that those who oppose you may be ashamed because they have nothing bad to say about us."[*]

"But the fruit of the Spirit is love, joy, peace, forbearance, kindness, goodness, faithfulness, gentleness and self-control. Against such things there is no law."[†]

"Whoever walks in integrity walks securely, but whoever takes crooked paths will be found out."[‡]

"For this very reason, make every effort to supplement your faith with virtue, and virtue with knowledge, and knowledge with self-control, and self-control with steadfastness, and steadfastness with godliness, and godliness with brotherly affection, and brotherly affection with love."[§]

---

[*]   Titus 2:7-8 NIV
[†]   Galatians 5:22-23 NIV
[‡]   Proverbs 10:9 NIV
[§]   2 Peter 1:5-7 ESV

"Put on then, as God's chosen ones, holy and beloved, compassionate hearts, kindness, humility, meekness, and patience, bearing with one another and, if one has a complaint against another, forgiving each other; as the Lord has forgiven you, so you also must forgive. And above all these put on love, which binds everything together in perfect harmony. And let the peace of Christ rule in your hearts, to which indeed you were called in one body. And be thankful."*

I could go on and on with a list of Scripture verses that emphasize the importance of character, but the most sobering one is this: "Beware of false prophets, who come to you in sheep's clothing but inwardly are ravenous wolves. You will recognize them by their fruits."†29

I need to pause here and point out how beautiful the prophetic is. I'm convinced that we all long in the depths of our being to hear Him, but many haven't been awakened to His voice that is all around us. He is speaking through our loved ones, through our circumstances, and through His creation every single day. He is inviting us to live our lives seeking His voice through every possible avenue, and we eagerly do so when we're in love.

If we become accustomed to finding Him moving and speaking through all possible avenues, then it will be easier to discern when He is speaking through a prophetic gift. The reality is that all prophetic words are a mixture. God's voice moves through our own voice, our personality, and our humanity. We put our fingerprints all over things. It is unavoidable. Sometimes it is okay, and sometimes it is not. This is why our humility and submission to the weighing process is so very important.

But we must also remember that God genuinely likes us. He chooses to speak through us, and He is not completely opposed to our involvement. He speaks what He speaks through us on purpose because our personality

---

*   Colossians 3:12-15 ESV
†   Matthew 7:15–16 ESV

and general DNA will be a good carrier for this or that particular message. I don't think we will ever completely get ourselves out of it, and I don't think that's the main point. It is up to us as the "testers and weighers" to be able to sort out prophetic words and respond with maturity.

— CHAPTER 9 —

The Healthy Prophetic Soul

Over the years, I've heard many people attempt to explain what prophetic maturity looks like, and most of what they say makes my head tilt a little. I've heard some say that it has to do with the level of revelation one receives, or that it is about the number of prophetic words someone gives in a certain year. I've heard others say that it has to do with whether someone gives local or national or global prophetic words, while others define it by the power or level of revelation, visitation, or encounter. But I don't see any of this in Scripture. To define maturity in any spiritual gift, we really must look to define the maturity level of the human being who is stewarding the gift.

Yes, there are specific things a prophetically gifted person needs to learn about his or her actual gifting, such as learning the ways of God at deeper levels and growing in sensitivity to the Holy Spirit. But the majority of learning and growth is more connected to how you steward the gift you've been given, how you carry this calling within your heart and soul, and how you navigate the unavoidable demands this places upon your character.

In many charismatic circles, there has been a temptation toward a spirituality that is disembodied. It is a mindset that somehow gives permission for people to be highly spiritual, powerfully gifted, and yet utterly toxic in their relationships. If we pursue any version of spirituality apart from the concrete love of others, the tangible expression of service, and the character formation that happens within community, we will be permissioning our life on this earth to be disconnected from the call to be transformed into the image of Christ.

As disciples of Jesus, we are to be followers of His life, His ways, and His love.

There is absolutely nothing within our discipleship that makes room for growing in spiritual experience while neglecting the transformation of our character. This is a dangerous trap, especially for highly charged, charismatic cultures that can tend toward mindsets that elevate spiritual encounters and neglect the weightier matters such as justice and mercy (Matthew 23:23). This is exactly what Jesus was referring to when He spoke to the Pharisees about only cleaning the outside of the cup (Matthew 23:25-26), and could lead to Gnostic-like belief patterns.

I'll say it again. Regardless of what gift you have, the maturity of that gift will be directly linked to the maturity of your character, your honesty, your humility, your authenticity, and your ability to love, which is all lived out through your relationships. To talk about defining maturity in a spiritual gift without addressing the health of a person's mind, will, emotions and how those play out in his or her life and relationships seems downright silly.

Our journey toward wholeness will directly affect every aspect of our ministry. For example, if people are dangerously disconnected from their own heart and the hearts of others, if they are unaware of their unhealthy patterns of control, or if they are neglecting to face their own desperate need for approval, then the prophetic ministry that is coming through them will be tainted. It is unavoidable.

Authenticity, Vulnerability and Teachability

Of course, this pursuit of wholeness is a lifelong journey. None of us have arrived at perfection, and all of us are on a never-ending pathway of learning and growing. This isn't a conversation about perfectionism or behavior modification; rather, it is a discussion about discipleship. And effective discipleship requires authenticity, vulnerability, and teachability.

The topic of authenticity is included because it is vital that we let ourselves be seen in truth. We don't want to hide behind falsehood, pretending that we're better than we are or deceiving others into thinking that we are spiritual giants. The prophetic is a powerful gift, and it is easy to veer toward grandiosity. The decision to remain connected to your truest self, to allow yourself to be seen in weakness, and not to permit yourself to hide behind a facade of any kind is vital for true growth. There is no maturity in falsehood. In fact, I would go so far as to say that falsehood is one of the defining markers of immaturity. There is only true growth in authenticity.

Let no one disqualify you, insisting on asceticism and worship of angels, going on in detail about visions, puffed up without reason by his sensuous mind, and not holding fast to the Head, from whom the whole body, nourished and knit together through its joints and ligaments, grows with a growth that is from God (Colossians 2:18-19 ESV).

There are many kinds of "growth" presented to us in churches today. But let's make sure we are growing with a growth that is from God.

This leads us to the topic of vulnerability. The prophetic is incredibly vulnerable, especially when the gift is lived through the raw, unguarded reality of connected authenticity. The nature of the prophetic should push people toward a courageous embrace of vulnerability in order to remain authentically connected humans. The work of remaining connected to our own hearts, connected to the Lord in a raw and unguarded way, and connected to other people in love is our daily invitation. The vulnerability of engaging our whole heart, compelled by love to give ourselves over to be a conduit of the Lord, is overwhelming at times. If that is not difficult enough, we must also allow ourselves to remain connected to the impact and effect the words we speak will have, while remaining connected to the people to whom we're speaking.

There is no way to do justice on this topic in just one chapter because it is filled with nuance on every possible level, but let me say that love is vulnerable. Love is authentic. And being transformed in and through love is the true journey of our life in Christ. So our pathway into maturity is rooted in our journey of learning how to love. "Pursue love, yet earnestly desire spiritual gifts, but especially that you may prophesy."*

The difference between pursuit and desire is monumental. We pursue love inwardly, reminding ourselves daily that our motive for everything is to be love. What we are connected to within ourselves is what will be released through us. Stewarding our heart is our most difficult task! But there will be no true demonstration of love if we don't first cultivate love within our own hearts. Then we pursue love outwardly by allowing our actions to demonstrate the love of Christ flowing through us authentically in all we do. This is our pursuit.

We must also talk about teachability. Only the teachable will grow deeply into maturity. Teachability is something we should never outgrow. Pride comes before the fall, because a prideful heart doesn't submit itself to being a forever learner. May we be quick to repent, easy to correct, moldable in our understanding, and childlike in our desire to learn.

Those who believe themselves to be experts have stopped growing and have ceased to be learners. In so doing, they have put a ceiling over their heads. Childlike humility will always lead us into opportunities to

---

*   1 Corinthians 14:1

learn and grow, but it will also require greater and greater humility. Our egos will tempt us toward overconfidence and presumption, which are killers of the true prophetic.

The Tension

For some odd reason, it is difficult for us to be both confident and humble, to be teachable and bold. Not to mention the battles we have with the fear of humans versus the fear of the Lord! The tensions between the fear of man and the desire to be socially appropriate are real. The pressure to please people in our culture is fierce. How do we navigate the waters of our heart as we pursue the holy tremble in obedience to our Lord and King, while at the same time love people in health and not in flattery? How do we spot the fear of man within our soul and hold our faces like flint gazing only at the glory of God?

Stewarding our hearts as we grow in the prophetic is not easy, but this is our call. The Lord calls us to lay ourselves bare and go boldly in faith as we speak what He is asking us to speak. He calls us to do exactly what He is asking us to do and to do it wholeheartedly and in humility, ready to be corrected, instructed, and submissive. It can sometimes feel like a tug-of-war within ourselves to navigate these waters, but we must.

Our humanity is like a pasta strainer. The Holy Spirit moves through our strainer/filter, influencing the prophecies flowing through us. We all have filters formed by our culture, by the trauma we have experienced, by our political or social leanings, and by our upbringing. Some of these filters can be harmless, depending on how directly they relate to the words the Lord is speaking. Other filters, however, can twist the words we're hearing into something that wasn't His intended meaning. I don't believe we will ever arrive at a point in which we will be prophesying one hundred percent fully divine. I believe it is always going to have some kind of mixture, and that is okay. The Lord knows this, and yet He still chooses to partner with us as weak and imperfect human beings. It is so stunning! "We are to grow up in all aspects into Him who is the head, that is, Christ."*

The journey of maturity within our soul is continually before us. It beckons us to steward our mind, will, and emotions well, daily surrendering all to the lordship of Christ. As we read the above passage in Ephesians, it is important that we pay attention to what directly follows:

"From whom the whole body, being fitted and held together by what every joint supplies, according to the proper working of each individual part, causes the growth of the body for the building up of itself in love ."†

Our path to maturity will always lead us and pull us together into community. There is no maturing outside of the Body of Christ. We grow together by learning to love each other, speaking truth to each other, and being formed together.

As we long to grow into maturity as prophetic people, we must grow in both God-awareness and self-awareness. It is so important that we learn how to reflect on the deep inner workings of our soul and how to observe the emotional twists and turns that are happening beneath the surface.

---

*   Ephesians 4:15
†   Ephesians 4:16

We must then do the work that is necessary to grow:

- Own your issues. No one else can be responsible for your emotional sin patterns. If you're going to prophesy, the most challenging work will be to recognize and own the issues that will become your filters.
- Repent for what needs repenting, and do it quickly.
- Get healing and counsel for what needs restoration, and don't delay.
- Remain in community with people who know you well and who will speak honestly into your life.
- Train your heart to submit to honest feedback. Receive it humbly and then make the changes required.
- Educate yourself on your cultural pitfalls, acknowledging where your culture has formed your paradigms. Do what needs to be done to broaden your perceptions.
- Pay attention to your desire for control, to your temptations toward toxic self protection, and to your ego that hungers for attention and validation. Respond with humility and teachability before the Lord.
- Keep your heart open. This is more difficult than it sounds! Keep your heart open toward God, toward people, and toward the pain of the world.
- Make no room for self-pity, victim mindsets, bitterness, etc. These will seriously damage the way you hear His voice.

Stand in Counsel

The best advice I can give on the journey toward a healthy selfawareness is to stand in the counsel of the Lord with an open heart, ready to see what He shows you about the state of your soul. Do this daily, and take your time with it. Then ask others to speak freely into your life. Ask for honest and difficult feedback. Make your heart a safe place for people to engage in hard conversations.

"The LORD confides in those who fear him; he makes his covenant known to them."[*]

"If I regard wickedness in my heart, the Lord will not hear."[†]

"In days to come you will understand it clearly. I did not send these prophets, yet they have run with their message; I did not speak to them, yet they have prophesied. But if they had stood in my council, they would have proclaimed my words to my people and would have turned them from their evil ways and from their evil deeds."[‡]

"When I tried to understand all this, it troubled me deeply till I entered the sanctuary of God."[§]

---

[*]   Psalm 25:14 NIV
[†]   Psalm 66:18 KJ21
[‡]   Jeremiah 23:20-22 NIV
[§]   Psalm 73:16-17 NIV

— CHAPTER 10 —

Anchored in the Eternal Story

Prophets are called to point. They are like an unrelenting signpost that never ceases to draw all people to the eternal purpose and perspective of God. They point toward God's desire to have a people who are in union with Himself. They point toward the longing of God for a Kingdom of priests who exemplify His purpose for humanity. They point toward the covenantal union that holds us together until the fullness of the Kingdom is manifested on the earth. They point in one direction and toward one end. The purpose of the prophetic is to tenaciously point toward the covenant that binds us to the eternal mission of Christ Jesus.

Prophets are the ones who have their eyes on the goal and their gaze fixed on the promise of a Kingdom not yet fully realized. They are called to continually hold within their view a vision of where this whole story is headed. It is as if prophets have their gaze set on the horizon, on the fixed point of our destination, and that vision informs everything about the message they carry in this present moment. Like Abraham who lived as an alien in the land of promise looking for the city whose architect and builder was God Himself (Hebrews 11), the prophetic call is more solidly anchored when a prophet has a healthy theological view of the whole God story.

This, of course, doesn't happen overnight. But I do believe it is imperative that prophetic people mature into being able to maintain a healthy big-picture understanding that gives them a firm grasp on where to point. Imagine the damage that could happen if they were to point in the wrong direction! If prophets lose their anchor on the eternal, if they allow their focus to be formed by worldly or self-centered paradigms, or worse yet, if they have a non-biblical end-time view of how this story is going to unfold, the prophetic gift moving through them would definitely be affected.

If a prophet was deceived by a theology that was heavily influenced by punitive judgment, how would this affect the prophetic words moving through him or her?

If a prophet had an escapist, an elitist, or a legalistic view of the world rather than a redemptive Kingdom view, how would that affect the prophetic moving through him or her?

If a prophet had a nationalistic paradigm, or if he or she believed that the Kingdom was to come through political means, elevating the powers of the age rather than the powers and purposes of the eternal Kingdom, how would this affect the prophetic moving through him or her?

Our twisted and ill-informed theological filters will cause us to misinterpret, misunderstand, and misapply the voice of God. My fear is that many prophetic people in the world today have been more formed by a series of End Times movies than by Scripture itself. That is, of course, if they have any eternal view whatsoever. In our current culture of immediacy, individualism, and self-centeredness, I sometimes wonder if we have lost the joy that is set before us.

A Look at Paul

> There are certain activities—music, mathematics, and chess, for instance—in
> which quite young people can become prodigies. In Jewish families, studying
> the Torah can be like that: the young mind and heart can drink it all in, sense its
> drama and rhythms, relish the ancestral story and promise. The youngster can
> get to know his way around the Five Books of Moses the way he knows the way
> around his own home. All the signs are that Saul of Tarsus was that kind of child.[30]

Paul the apostle was nurtured and raised in a truly zealous faith in the
house of Pharisees. Their covenant with God was the absolute center of
their culture, and it utterly defined every aspect of their way of life. Brilliant
students like Paul would have soaked in, meditated on, and memorized
the Old Testament stories of Yahweh. He would have likely gone to bed
dreaming about the story of the Throne Room (Isaiah 6), of Elijah on
the mountaintop defeating Baal (1 Kings 18), and of Ezekiel's encounter
with the Holy One of Israel (Ezekiel 1-2). Passionate Jews like Paul would
have lived and breathed the fear of the Lord. They lived in the tremble of
the Holy One they worshiped, with their eyes fixed upon the promised
Kingdom to come.

The entirety of the Jewish way of life centered around the temple. This
building made with hands had been consecrated by heaven in a powerful
demonstration of God's infilling (2 Chronicles 7), making it clear that this
temple was now God's dwelling place on earth. This building was the
meeting place between heaven and earth. On that fateful Damascus road,
Saul/Paul was on a zealous mission to guard and protect this temple and
anything that would lead his people away from Yahweh.

We need to remember that Saul did not have a conversion experience.
He wasn't indoctrinated into a new religion. He wasn't reasoned with in
order to accept Jesus into his heart. He didn't go to school in order to
learn how to be a strong Christian. He didn't have an evangelist walk him

through Scripture in order to understand the steps of salvation. As Jesus encountered Saul on that day, surrounded by blinding light, Saul had to reconcile that the Holy Temple, the meeting place of heaven and earth, was now inside of this Man. He realized that what had once sounded to his ears as blasphemy was true. He encountered the Person, and he was utterly captured by Christ.

We have no idea just how many revelations went through Saul's mind in that moment. He came face to face with the Messiah for whom he had been desperately searching, and he found out that he was actually persecuting the God he served. In one single moment, his entire world changed.

And because of this encounter and his subsequent transformation, he lost everything. He would have been exiled from his family. He would have lost his friends, his community, and the career he had pursued aggressively his entire life. But there was no going back. He had met the Messiah. He had encountered the King of the Kingdom. This was the One he had been dreaming of and envisioning his whole life.

What kind of faith and what focus of heart dwells within the man who penned these words?

"Christ will even now, as always, be exalted in my body, whether by life or by death. For to me, to live is Christ, and to die is gain."*

"I have been crucified with Christ; and it is no longer I who live, but Christ lives in me."†

It was the kind of man who described himself as "Paul, a bond-servant of God and an apostle of Jesus Christ, for the faith of those chosen of God and the knowledge of the truth which is according to godliness, in the hope of eternal life."‡ Paul's faith was not passive. He was not waiting for some glorious by-and-by. He didn't have a heaven that would take him

---

* Phillippians 1:20-21
† Galatians 2:20
‡ Titus 1:1-2

away from this world, floating up into the clouds to live a utopian afterlife. Neither was his faith one that preached a goal of inner peace, personal piety, or spiritual mastery. Paul's life was a demonstration of someone who was fully awakened to the hope that is set before us, with a true vision of the Kingdom of heaven manifested on earth.

Eternal Vision

We must anchor ourselves in the eternal purposes of Christ. We are living a story that is headed somewhere. There is a vision, there is a goal, and there is a purpose to it all. And for the prophetic person in particular, the eternal vision, the reason for the covenant, and the fulfillment of the Kingdom is to be deeply intertwined with all that he or she prophecies.

In Hebrews 11, the great hall of faith, we see these astonishing men and women who are forever exalted in the eyes of God because of their courageous acts of faith. But where did this faith come from? In what was their faith anchored?

"By faith he [Abraham] lived as a stranger in the land of promise... for he was looking for the city which has foundations, whose architect and builder is God."*

"And what more shall I say? For time will fail me if I tell of Gideon, Barak, Samson, Jephthah, of David and Samuel and the prophets, who by faith conquered kingdoms, performed acts of righteousness, obtained promises, shut the mouths of lions, quenched the power of fire, escaped the edge of the sword, from weakness were made strong, became mighty in war, put foreign armies to flight. Women received back their dead by resurrection; and others were tortured, not accepting their release, so that they might obtain a better resurrection; and others experienced mocking and flogging, and further, chains and imprisonment. They were stoned,

---

* Hebrews 11:9-10

they were sawn in two, they were tempted, they were put to death with the sword; they went about in sheepskins, in goatskins, being destitute, afflicted, tormented (people of whom the world was not worthy), wandering in deserts, on mountains, and sheltering in caves and holes in the ground. And all these, having gained approval through their faith, did not receive what was promised, because God had provided something better for us."*

"Having confessed that they were strangers and exiles on the earth."†

"They desire a better country, that is, a heavenly one. Therefore God is not ashamed to be called their God; for He has prepared a city for them."‡

"All these died in faith, without receiving the promises, but having seen and welcomed them from a distance, and having confessed that they were strangers and exiles on the earth. For those who say such things make it clear that they are seeking a country of their own. And indeed if they had been thinking of that country which they left, they would have had opportunity to return. But as it is, they desire a better country, that is, a heavenly one. Therefore God is not ashamed to be called their God; for He has prepared a city for them."§

These men and women who stand as beacons of light and strength in our Christian lineage all have one thing in common: they were single-minded. They had hearts that were captured by Christ, and they had a view fixed on eternity. We are living in the most impatient culture of all of human history. Has this influenced our theology? Have we sacrificed the importance of a faith that is rooted and anchored in the eternal Kingdom for the sake of our immediate wants, needs, and fleshly desires? Could this possibly be the cause of our hope deferred?

As I've heard the stories of the saints who walked through persecution, I have noticed that the same thread runs through each one: their

---

* Hebrews 11:32-40
† Hebrews 11:13
‡ Hebrews 11:16
§ Hebrews 11:13-16

eyes were fixed on the goal. They could see the promised Kingdom as if it was right in front of them. Their eternal perspective became an anchor that held them through every storm. They had a hunger and thirst for the eternal that birthed true anticipation. They could endure anything on this earth as they looked to the joy set before them. No one could harm their untouchable destiny. They saw themselves as undeserving sinners who were caught up in the beauty and the grace of what was promised to them. They embraced their destiny in eternity with a passion that pulled them through the shadow of the valley of death. They could endure. They could even find peace and joy in the trial, because they could see the fullness of the Kingdom with a prophetic imagination.

But remember the former days, when, after being enlightened, you endured a great conflict of sufferings, partly by being made a public spectacle through insults and distress, and partly by becoming companions with those who were so treated. For you showed sympathy to the prisoners and accepted joyfully the seizure of your property, knowing that you have for yourselves a better and lasting possession (Hebrews 10:32-34).

Pause for a moment to really think about this. They accepted the seizure of their property? Joyfully? Can you imagine? Of course, this is the faith that all followers of Jesus are called to grow in. But as prophetic people who are called to point to the eternal purposes of God and who are to call His children back into right relationship with the King of heaven, this aspect of our faith is immutable.

The Call

> They seemed to be standing in the courts of heaven with eyes seeing a different reality, ears tuned to a different dimension, and hearts pounding with a different purpose from the rest of us. It is as if they physically felt every crack that could bring Israel into disharmony with God, and it was unbearable to them.[31]

This is the call. This is what our eyes must be trained in. There are many ministries that try to teach people how to see into the realm of the spirit. They try to train people to see angels and demons and to have spiritual encounters. I honestly don't see this being a focus of the teachings of Scripture. I do, however, see how Paul had his eyes fixed on the eternal Kingdom in such a way that it spilled over into much of what he wrote. It drove his every action toward one goal: the eternal purpose and glory of Christ.

> "For we know that the whole creation groans and suffers the pains of childbirth together until now. And not only this, but also we ourselves, having the first fruits of the Spirit, even we ourselves groan within ourselves, waiting eagerly for our adoption as sons, the redemption of our body."[*]

> "Therefore if you have been raised up with Christ, keep seeking the things above, where Christ is, seated at the right hand of God. Set your minds on the things above, not on the things that are on earth."[†]

---

[*]   Romans 8:22-23
[†]   Colossians 3:1-2

— CHAPTER 11 —

The Five Fold

In the discussion of the prophetic it's nearly impossible to ignore what is commonly called the fivefold ministry gifts. There is no way to do this topic justice in just one chapter, but I will do my best to skim some of the major themes, leaving room for differing theologies, viewpoints and honoring the place of mystery.

Ephesians 4 is the primary passage that discusses the fivefold gifts. In this chapter, we will take a look at these passages and discuss a few elements that feel important. But first, let's look at some nuances about various kinds of prophetic gifting found in Scripture. These nuances are seemingly subtle, but they're worth mentioning up front and then describing in more detail later in this chapter.

Not all prophetically gifted people are called to be prophets in the way that Ephesians 4 depicts. I once heard an analogy that works quite well to describe the subtleties of this point. We are all able to run—especially if there is danger chasing us! Some, however, run on a regular basis for exercise. And still others receive the title of "runners." The act of running is the same, but the way it's carried, or embodied is different. It is similar with the prophetic.

We can all prophesy—and some find themselves prophesying quite often—but others are actual prophets. Not everyone who prophesies has a call on their lives that brings the weight we see in Ephesians 4:11. The act of prophesying is the same, but God utilizes it in people differently. The end goal, however, is still the same. Whether you're a prophet, prophetically gifted, or just find yourself prophesying sometimes, most of the purposes discussed in Ephesians 4 still pertain to you.

As we take a look at Ephesians 4, we will begin with verse 10. It says that Christ "ascended far above all the heavens, that He might fill all things." God's intention, His mission and purpose, is to pursue the whole world with His love, filling it all with His presence. God's passionate desire to dwell with us and fill the whole world with His glory is the story of the Bible from beginning to end.

"But truly, as I live, and as all the earth shall be filled with the glory of the LORD."*

"Blessed be his glorious name forever; may the whole earth be filled with his glory! Amen and Amen!"†

And the end goal:

"And I heard a loud voice from the throne saying, "Look! God's dwelling place is now among the people, and he will dwell with them. They will be his people, and God himself will be with them and be their God."‡

"Christ in you, the hope of glory."§

The Church's primary call is to accomplish the mission of the Lord, fulfilling the dream of God to see the world filled with His presence through the Gospel of Jesus Christ. David Bosch, the seminal missiologist, said in his book Transforming Mission, "It is not true that there is a mission because there is a church. Rather, there is a church because there is a mission."[32] The Church is the carrier of the mission of God. Whether

---

*   Numbers 14:21 ESV
†   Psalm 72:19 ESV
‡   Revelation 21:3 NIV
§   Colossians 1:27 ESV

we like it or not, the Church is plan A. There is no plan B. Scholars have sometimes referred to the whole book of Ephesians as the constitutional treatise of Paul to the Church at large. The fivefold passages are found in the middle of Paul laying out some heavy-duty spiritual architecture for the establishment of the Church. The conversation of the fivefold should never be divorced from the conversation of the establishment of the big C Church.

"So then you are no longer strangers and foreigners, but you are fellow citizens with the saints, and are of God's household, having been built on the foundation of the apostles and prophets, Christ Jesus Himself being the cornerstone, in whom the whole building, being fitted together, is growing into a holy temple in the Lord, in whom you also are being built together into a dwelling of God in the Spirit."*

The primary role of apostles and prophets is to lay the foundation for the building and maturing of the Church. This would be one of the roles of a prophet that would differ from someone who finds themselves prophesying sometimes. Not everyone who prophesies carries the weight of laying foundations. But everyone who prophecies should still carry the passion for "the household of God to grow into a holy temple in the Lord." Everyone who prophesies should at least have a vision for the big C Church "being built together into a dwelling place for God by the Spirit." In fact, this vision is what we are all called to aim our lives toward. Even though church is a complicated place for many people, and the human condition makes this a very messy journey, my prayer is that every prophetically gifted person will carry within their hearts a revelation of the spiritual Body of Christ in the earth. This is what will hold our feet to the fire and keep us from either walking away or building our own kingdom.

---

*   Ephesians 2:19-22

As Ephesians 4 continues, Paul lists the five. "He gave some as apostles, some as prophets, some as evangelists, some as pastors [or shepherds] and teachers" (verse 11). Paul paints a verbal picture of Jesus ascending to take His place as King. In His wake, He gives certain people as gifts to the Church. The subject He is emphatic in Greek to denote that Christ, Himself, gives these specific gifts. This language is different from what is used in 1 Corinthians 12 where we read that spiritual gifts are given by the Holy Spirit to all believers. It is important to note that the gifts in Ephesians 4 are the people themselves. These specifically gifted people are His gift to the Church to accomplish His designed purposes. In verse 7, Paul says: "To each one of us grace was given according to the measure of Christ's gift." Some take this to mean that every believer has some element of one or more of these five graces. This, however, is different wording than we read in verse 11 when he says, "He gave some as...."

There are, of course, many different ways that people understand this passage. Even among those who believe in the present-day operation of the gifts of the Spirit, there are many varying interpretations of this Ephesians 4 passage. Some have come to pretty dramatic conclusions about what this passage suggests, grabbing hold of the idea of "offices" to validate extremely high levels of unchecked authority.

Others take what they read in this one verse to define what the entire structure of the Church is supposed to be built upon. These interpretations are understandable, to a point, because the language here is clearly governmental in nature. But it can be dangerous to become too rigid in our interpretation and application based on one verse alone. We must take Scripture as a whole, bringing in other relevant passages for consideration.

It is also true that many people today, having been hurt or disillusioned by the sorts of imbalanced applications mentioned above, have simply rejected the concept of the fivefold altogether. I would say, however, that such reactions are equally inadvisable. It would be a grave mistake to ignore this verse when having discussions of oversight, guidance, and foundation-building for the Church. I am convinced that the healthy functioning of these five gifts is essential for the Body of Christ to become mature. But what does this actually look like? That's the difficult question. Let's take a look at the surrounding context of this passage.

"I therefore, a prisoner for the Lord, urge you to walk in a manner worthy of the calling to which you have been called, with all humility and gentleness, with patience, bearing with one another in love, eager to maintain the unity of the Spirit in the bond of peace."*

> The first thing we should notice is that when Paul says, therefore, at the beginning of this passage, he means "in light of the glorious gospel which I have just proclaimed to you" (in the first three chapters of the epistle). This is important because it means that everything that follows from these verses is framed as the right response to the Good News of the Gospel of Jesus Christ.[33]

This validates that we cannot separate the prophetic calling from the call to emanate the character of Christ. Paul lists humility and gentleness, patience, bearing with one another in love, while remaining eager to maintain unity, as if to put first things first.

> This is the context, the foundation: the gospel message of reconciliation with God and with one another, in and through Jesus Christ, received and responded to in the manner described.[34]

And he gave the apostles, the prophets, the evangelists, the shepherds [or pastors] and teachers, to equip the saints for the work of ministry, for building up the body of Christ, until we all attain to the unity of the faith and of the knowledge of the Son of God, to mature manhood, to the measure of the stature of the fullness of Christ, so that we may no longer

---

* Ephesians 4:1-3 ESV

be children, tossed to and fro by the waves and carried about by every wind of doctrine, by human cunning, by craftiness in deceitful schemes. Rather, speaking the truth in love, we are to grow up in every way into him who is the head, into Christ, from whom the whole body, joined and held together by every joint with which it is equipped, when each part is working properly, makes the body grow so that it builds itself up in love (Ephesians 4:11-16 ESV).

The number one thing I want to highlight is that each of these five gifts/offices and/or callings share one common purpose. They are all pointing in the same direction, on the same mission. As we've discussed throughout this book, the purpose of the prophetic is primary. If we don't know the purpose of a thing, we are destined to abuse it. The five gifts mentioned in this famous passage share a common purpose.

> This is the essence of a truly New Testament understanding of what
> 'spiritual formation' is really about—each and every member of the
> Body of Christ, united with one another, growing up into matu-
> rity, and becoming all that we were destined to be… together.
> …for building up the Body of Christ…
> …until we all attain to the the unity of the faith and of the
> knowledge of the Son of God…to mature manhood, to the
> measure of the stature of the fullness of Christ…
> …so that we may no longer be children, tossed to and fro by the waves…
> …we are to grow up in every way into Him who is the head, into Christ…
> …the whole body, joined and held together by every joint with
> which it is equipped… when each part is working properly…
> …the body grow so that it builds itself up in love.[35]

It's very easy to lose sight of this purpose and make the various functions of these unique gifts an end unto themselves. In the Church today, it's commonplace to see these gifts siloed in their own separate arenas, pursuing their own passions and purposes. For instance, how often have you heard it said that prophets and pastors are always at odds with one another, always disagreeing about where the church's focus should be? The stereotypes would say that pastors are commonly described as only caring about "tending the flock" with little regard for what the Holy Spirit is saying or doing, while prophets are often portrayed as thinking only about spiritual realities with no time to care about the practical, physical, and emotional needs of those in their Church family.

These are exaggerations, of course. But I do think there is a near segregation between these five callings in many churches today. We see evangelists, teachers, pastors, prophets, and apostles seemingly doing their own ministries with their own emphasis, disconnected from the other parts of the fivefold. What would it look like to see these five gifts working together toward the common purposes listed in this passage?

> One thing Paul makes plain in this passage is that the proper functioning of these five gifts together is God's sovereignly ordained means for bringing about His purpose for the Church. While we must be very careful not to become dogmatic about our particular interpretation of the unique functions of each of these gifts, or about what kinds of ecclesiastical structures best facilitate their working together, I think we can say with confidence based on the text that we must have these gifts functioning together if we are to fulfill God's purpose for us in this world.[36]

The fivefold has a purpose. The prophetic has a purpose that is connected to the fivefold. We need the fivefold gifts primarily because we need the outcomes described in Ephesians 4:13-16. If we pursue the "offices" without the goal, the intent, or the passion for the outcomes, then we have missed the point entirely. A fivefold ministry that does not expect to see unity, Christlikeness, fewer deceived believers, and a Body that is built up in love and is maturely living out the Gospel of the Kingdom is at risk of being self-indulgent.

I can't imagine how the isolated prophet with his or her individual ministry could accomplish his or her true, biblical purpose. The one shared purpose of these callings puts a demand upon prophets to work in union with the rest of the five (and others), and in ongoing relationship with the communities they are influencing.

A sports team is made up of various positions and players, each with their own role and function, but all work together for the same goal. In the same way, an orchestra is composed of many musicians playing different instruments, but each must work in harmony with the others in order to bring forth beautiful music. The gifts of Christ and of the Spirit will not accomplish their intended purpose if they are not working hand in hand with the other gifts. It is a brilliantly designed organism created by God to build, nurture and equip the Church to become all that it is destined to be.

CHAPTER 12

The Prophetic in the Local Church

If you are carrying a prophetic gift inside of you, please remember that it is holy and beautiful, but it is not simple or easy to carry well. This gift belongs to the Lord and is given to you to co-steward. It is a gift that we have been entrusted to host within our souls. It is holy and powerful and yet moves through our broken and imperfect lives. It feels heavy sometimes, like it could actually crush us. But at other times, it catches us up into the glory of His presence in ways that are indescribable. It is a gift that comes with a cost. We will often feel the pain of the world.

We will sometimes feel the brokenness of humanity in our bones. We will make massive mistakes and feel humiliated—I think it's unavoidable.

We will experience a level of vulnerability we never knew existed, finding ourselves connecting emotionally with the nakedness of Isaiah. We will do things while under His anointing and then want to hide away for days because of how exposed we feel. We will want to run away, and sometimes we will. But His love won't let us go too far. We will feel alienated, misunderstood, and weirdly exalted. We will see the pride that crouches in the shadows and comes out to bite us when we least expect it.

We need community.

I cannot emphasize strongly enough how vital it is for all prophetically gifted people to be deeply rooted in the life of a local church. The call to make disciples implicitly includes the call to be disciples—to be apprenticed and trained—and those who are prophetically gifted or even called to be prophets are in no way exempt from this call to mutual submission and corporate discipleship. We are to be known, nurtured, taught, and formed by active participation in a believing community.

There is honestly no way to escape this in Scripture. I hope that at this point in this book this foundation has become abundantly clear. Even people who have a national or global prophetic call on their lives are to be anchored in a local community where they're known, submitted, challenged, and cared for. This doesn't ever change. The local church is where we grow, mature, practice, and stretch our gifting. It is also the primary place where the prophetic gift functions to help guide, inspire, and align the Kingdom of God through a life-giving body of local believers. But it is messy. Oh, so very messy.

What we must remember is that within the mess is our most valuable transformation. In the end, our life journey is more about being transformed into His image than it is about the prophetic gift. It is amazing how easy it is to forget this truth. So we must hold it intentionally central in our view so that it can inform us every day. If we know that our transformation into His image is more important than this prophetic gift or calling, then we will not become confused about our participation within the local church.

A healthy local church will form us into who He wants us to be. When we give ourselves to a loving and healthy community, we are anchored in ways that are hard to describe. The church disciples our heart and keeps us accountable to Scripture. Submitting our hearts to be loved, corrected, and instructed by those who deeply know us will nurture more growth in our gift than any conference or course ever could. As we're surrounded by community, we are seen as a whole person and not just a gift. It is here that we learn to receive correction well. We learn how to be weak and frail while still powerful and anointed. We need a place to run when we feel rejected, judged, and torn down. We need a safe place to be held.

Learning how to handle the spotlight and embrace the seasons of hiddenness is crucial. This takes community. This takes being pastored. I promise you that anchoring your heart within a vulnerable, authentic community will be the hardest thing you do, but nothing will be more empowering. Even though it will feel disempowering at times.

As we've studied the prophetic throughout Scripture, you have undoubtedly felt the tremble. But this calling isn't just rising to the heights of bringing the full word of the Lord in power and boldness. It is also calling us lower to the ground in humility and submission, trust and self-sacrifice, with hearts that are sliced open in vulnerability and surrender. The latter will actually be the greater calling than the former as you stand before His throne.

We can't do this alone.

My Advice

If you feel you have a prophetic call on your life, I would recommend you build a strong, trusted relationship with your pastor and/or leaders. The relationship between pastor and prophet is complex but essential. As you build trust with your leader(s), let them see you. Let them see your heart, your weaknesses, and your struggles. Let them in. Then ask them if they can still trust your gift through your weaknesses.

Ask them if they will help you grow, and then trust yourself into their care. Tell them that you want to be able to receive correction in a healthy way. Tell them that you welcome others testing and weighing the prophetic words that come through you and that you desire to learn from this process. If you don't feel this is possible, then please seek counsel to discern why. Your gift can't function in health if you can't trust your leaders. If your leaders are untrustworthy with your heart, then you have a much bigger conversation that needs to happen.

Remember The Purpose

As we've observed the prophetic gift functioning in a variety of places throughout Scripture—the Old Testament prophets, the life of David, the ministry of Jesus, and all throughout the New Testament—how can we not be struck with awe and wonder about the diversity of it all? Each and every prophet had a different style, personality, expression, passion, etc. Their specific assignments were varied, but we can see a clear and discernable common thread of purpose and focus running through each one that wove them all together. From start to finish, we can see the purpose of the prophetic gift: to communicate God's inspired declaration, calling the sons and daughters of the Kingdom into alignment with His covenant purpose in Christ.

Remember those who have become experts at spotting counterfeit currency? They are trained by intensively studying, handling, memorizing, gazing at, and becoming intimately familiar with the real currency. In this way, they become able to easily spot that which is not real the moment they come into contact with it. Together, we have endeavored to observe, study, gaze upon, and contemplate the real in the hope of reorienting our paradigms toward the true prophetic purpose as it has been revealed in Scripture.

The pastoral part of me wants to sit down with you and ask you about your local church context. What kind of experiences have you had with the prophetic? Have you had past experiences that are currently hindering you? This is so often the case. There is much misunderstanding of the prophetic. In some circles, it is viewed as harsh, corrective, and downright scary. In other circles, it is viewed as bubble gum and candy sprinkles that are sent to make us feel good about ourselves.

Many prophetic people I know are wounded. I take great comfort in the fact that the prophets in Scripture were probably wounded, too. They certainly suffered more rejection and misunderstanding than many of us have. My greatest hope for you is that you have healthy, trustworthy leaders with whom you feel safe enough to be vulnerable and find healing.

In this book, I have attempted to lift off the glass ceiling from the prophetic, while at the same time deepening our root system into humility, accountability, and community. This is a high call that puts a great demand on our spiritual, emotional, and relational maturity. I hope and pray that you have a healthy place where you can grow in all of these ways.

I've written this next section as a personal letter to all Pastors and Leaders of local churches.

Can we imagine together?

What would it look like to have mature, healthy, humble prophets who are standing in their place, anchored in a community where they are known, loved, received, and cared for.

What would it look like for these prophets to submit themselves joyfully to healthy leaders who watch over their lives, guiding, teaching, and correcting them in love and receiving their gift in all its stages, even when it's messy?

What would it look like for confident, humble pastors and leaders who know how to steward the prophetic in their community, working together with elders, intercessors, and discerners as each person offers his or her part?

What would it look like for these communities to be filled with people who understand the prophetic calling and who know how to relate to these prophetically gifted people in healthy ways?

This is what we need to see in order for the prophetic mature in it's rightful calling and drawing His Church into alignment with Jesus Christ and His eternal purposes.

This book and the ReFraming the Prophetic course have been written to help create a pathway that leads to this joyful goal. Within the local church, we see three specific building blocks that are needed to nurture us toward prophetic health: Foundation, Framework, and Function.

Foundation

Laying the foundation for the prophetic within your local community begins with education.

I believe that no church community will be able to mature in the prophetic unless the leaders themselves continue to grow their understanding of this gift and its purpose. If our leaders don't have a healthy theology and understanding of the prophetic that empowers them to confidently pursue and steward the fullness of the prophetic in their midst, things will not go well.

We need to invest deeply in the hearts and lives of those who are prophetically gifted. The prophetic gift is to be honored but not exalted, desired but not chased after, and received joyfully while also tested seriously. People come to your community from so many different backgrounds and experiences—some healthy and some unhealthy. Offering training that will orient your prophetically gifted people around healthy scriptural paradigms will help unify a common understanding throughout your community.

That is the goal for which this book was written and for which the entire Reframing the Prophetic course was developed. The full ReFraming course is meant to be facilitated in group conversation offering a safe place for people to wrestle through their previously constructed paradigms. A secondary benefit of these types of dialogical learning environments is that they provide much-needed space for prophetically gifted individuals to spend time together, sharpening one another through the outworking of group biblical reflection. Unfortunately, people who function with this gift often become alienated for a number of reasons, and it is essential that we do everything we can to keep this from happening.

I also believe that it's important to teach the whole community how to relate to the prophetic. Every prophetic moment involves both the speaker and the hearer. Almost every prophetic "horror story" that I have heard involves mistakes that were made by both the giver and the receiver. This is why it is important to have regular teachings for the broader community about how to relate to the prophetic. They should be taught how to test and weigh prophetic words and how to seek and honor the voice of the Lord through others while feeling empowered with their yes or no.

Training and maturing our church communities in the practice of discernment is becoming more and more crucial. If we do not intentionally cultivate a healthy, biblical prophetic culture, another culture will form, and it probably won't be healthy. Culture always develops, so let's be intentional.

Framework

Building the framework entails putting some structure in place so the prophetic has a predetermined pathway for health and growth.

The practical outpouring of the prophetic gift in the local church usually moves in one of four expressions, although this varies greatly from church to church.

- Submitted Words: Words that are submitted to leadership teams from individual people--including possible direction, correction, warning or intercession—in order to aid and assist the leaders in their decision-making.
- Person-to-Person: Words that are given from one individual to another for the purpose of encouraging, guiding, and empowering the receiver in his or her walk with the Lord.
- Small Gatherings: Words that are delivered in the context of a small group of gathered believers (home groups, prayer gatherings, etc.) who have come together to seek the Lord.
- Large Gatherings: Words that are delivered in the context of larger corporate gatherings during which the Holy Spirit may be speaking a

word for the whole church community.

So, let's think through various scenarios and offer some ideas for a framework that will strengthen and support a healthy prophetic culture. Establishing a structure for how the prophetic can best operate in small and large gathering spaces (and person-to-person prophetic moments within those spaces) can be very helpful. In every setting, it's important to value the voice of God through the lives of the people present. These questions may help you get started on how to best set up a framework in your local community.

How do I need to equip my community so that there can be high levels of health and humility in person-to-person prophetic moments and sharing?

- How do I equip my leaders to be able to steward prophetic moments in their small groups, prayer meetings, etc.?
- How do we want to steward the prophetic in our larger gatherings?
- When someone believes they have a prophetic word, how, where, and with whom should they share this?
- What is the discernment process for when and how to share that word?
- If the word feels as if it is from the Lord but is not to be given at the moment, what happens to that word?

While small gathering spaces might look quite different from one another and have their unique structure, in large gathering spaces, it is a good idea to have a couple of people appointed to whom people can go if they have something to share with the whole community. Then the leaders of that gathering will discern what to do from there.

Establishing a Process for Submitted Words

Establishing a standard procedure for how to receive submitted prophetic words is key to building a framework for the prophetic in the local church. Prophetic environments are often expected to be in the moment or spontaneous, but arguably the most important words will never see the stage. These words might include direction, correction, warning, and intercession, and will be important for leaders to receive and steward. We'd like to encourage you to establish a process for how words can be submitted, discerned, distributed, and documented.

Submitted

Where can people send their words? The first thing we recommend is having a specific place (email address, etc.) for these words to be submitted. It's also a good idea to encourage people in your community to pray and listen to the Lord on behalf of the church, the city, the region, etc. If they believe they have heard the Lord, encourage them to write up what they believe the Lord has revealed to them and submit it through the process.

Discerned

What will then be done with this word? Who will test and weigh this word? When these submissions come in, we suggest you give them to a specific team that is trained and prepared to discern prophetic words together. We have called this our "discernment team." There is more on establishing a discernment team below.

Distributed

Who will decide what to do in response to this word? We propose that after the discernment team prays, weighs, and discerns, they pass on the words that feel as if they carry the Lord's voice to the leadership team—including their feedback and input about the words shared. As you have learned in this book, it is up to the leaders of churches to decide the final interpretation and application of the prophetic words given. So we ask our discernment team to refrain from being prescriptive regarding the application. We also ask the church leadership to take the application seriously, deciding upon what action needs to be taken. Does this word need to be shared with others (oversight, leaders, prayer teams, worship teams, the whole community, etc.)? When and how is best for this word to be shared? Does this word need to be saved for continued reflection? How does this word affect our current and future decisions?

Documented

Do you have some way to document words that have been received that are for a future time? It's very important that we document the words the Lord has spoken. If we truly believe God is speaking, then we need to take His words seriously. As we see throughout Scripture, the prophetic rarely works within our expected time frame. Sometimes the Lord speaks a few years in advance, other times He speaks for generations that are yet to be born. In our impatient culture of immediacy and instant gratification, it's easy to forget this!

If a word is given that feels as if it is for a time yet to come, we need to have some kind of structure in place that can help us to remember the words that we're still holding in prayer. We suggest establishing a system where people can revisit submitted, discerned, and distributed words at a later time. Additionally, documenting any fulfillment of those words is an incredible way to pass along the history of God's movement in our midst. It gives the powerful gift of a documented family heritage to the generations that come after us.

The questions of how to best submit, discern, distribute, and document words will be answered differently within every community, and those methods are influenced by the size of gatherings as well as the fluency of the spiritual gifts. Remember, there is rarely any urgency or rush with the prophetic. Taking time to send the words through a process of testing and weighing can only be of benefit to all.

Establishing a Discernment Team

All believers are able to discern. But more than that, we are all urged by the Scripture to mature in discernment. Yet, like many of the other spiritual gifts, the Holy Spirit has empowered some to carry this gift in a greater measure. It is a rare thing for the gifted discerners in our midst to have a space to intentionally use their gift within the Body of Christ, and this is unfortunate. Pulling a few people together who are gifted in discernment for the purpose of training them in a biblical understanding of both the prophetic gift and biblical discernment can help to empower them unto maturity.

We also believe that creating and nurturing a discernment team can be hugely helpful when it comes to testing and weighing submitted prophetic words. This is not only helpful for testing to see if a given word is from the Lord, but also for discerning possible ways to respond to such words. Ideally, such teams will be composed of people who are different from one another in various ways, because there is such great strength in diversity of perspective.

Function

Cultivating a culture for the function of the prophetic is done through intentional, trusting relationships.

The outworking of the function of the prophetic begins and ends in relationship. Here, we are focusing on the relationship between the pastors/elders/leaders, the discernment team members, and the prophetically gifted people in their midst. Rules and boundaries without relationship breed contempt and mistrust. Clearly communicated values that reinforce a healthy culture enable you to have a simplified structure. Everything we are discussing in this document can only be walked out in the context of a trusted relationship.

As church leaders in a local community, you are empowered to nurture this culture so that the prophetic can function in health and maturity. I encourage you to get to know and shepherd the prophetically gifted people in your midst. See them. Know their hearts. Be in their lives. Set the DNA of intentionality and trust. The strength of your partnership together gives way for the Holy Spirit to move most freely. You will know the best way to invest and nurture these specific relationships within your community. I believe in you as you intentionally cultivate a culture for the function of the prophetic to grow and for the purposes of Christ to be revealed.

I do understand the complexity of leading the prophetic in the local church, and my team and I are here to help. Our heart's desire is for whole, healthy churches, as I'm sure yours is as well. Please feel free to reach out to us for one-on-one conversations, questions, or coaching as you continue to steward the prophetic in your local community.

Dear Companions,

Since this is the end of this book, I want to take a moment to honor our journey together. Throughout these pages, we've covered a lot of ground! Each topic can feel a bit like drinking through a fire hose because we're covering so much material, and yet we often hear from our readers that they could spend months and months on each and every subject. We recognize that there is so much more to see of what Scripture teaches us about the prophetic gift and calling.

I would love to invite you to join a live cohort that offers further study on many of these topics. I have developed an entire 14-week course also entitled ReFraming the Prophetic. When you take part in the ReFraming the Prophetic course, you will dive in more deeply to the topics covered in this book as well as receive further insights and teachings from 23 different theologians, pastors, teachers, and missionaries from around the world. The course is run in an online cohort where you will journey with a small group of people internationally, diving into deep conversations and exploration of the prophetic. In these groups, you'll have the opportunity to discuss things such as:

- How did your heart respond to the Old Testament prophets as we looked at their humanity?
- What was your mind doing as we discussed David and the expansiveness of the prophetic arts?
- What did you see about Jesus as we looked at Him as our prophetic mentor that maybe you had never seen before?

- What did the Holy Spirit do within you as we pondered the experiences of Ananias, Saul, Cornelius, and Peter, or as we read the book of Acts and saw the prophetic in action?
- What did you glean from your study of the fivefold, the stewardship of power, and living life with an eternal perspective?
- How did you feel as you pondered the need for a healthy soul, learned how to test and weigh, and saw the beauty of an open and vulnerable posture within the local church?

Taking time to reflect on these topics with others will help to solidify what the Holy Spirit has done within you. To find out more about the course, please visit https://www.reframingtheprophetic.com/

Thank you so much for reading this book. We hope that it has been an enriching journey between you and the Lord. Please know that our team is accessible, and we would love to hear from you with any testimonies, thoughts, feedback or questions.

Your voice matters, email us at admin@reframingtheprophetic.com

Many blessings,

Christine Westhoff

Notes

1   David Foster Wallace, "This is Water: Commencement Speech at Kenton College," FS.blog, 2005, https://fs.blog/david-foster-wallace-this-is-water/.

2   "If You Understand, It is Not God," VerbumBible.com, April 9, 2019, https://verbumbible.com/2019/04/09/if-you-understand-it-is-not-god/

3   Abraham Heschel, The Prophets (New York: Harper Collins, 2001), introduction x

4   The male specific language appears unhelpful biblically since there were female prophets in the OT and also NT.

5   Heschel, introduction xiii

6   Ibid., 6.

7   Ibid.

8   Heschel, 25.

9   Ibid., 3

10   Ibid., 3

11   Heschel, 22.

12   Abraham Heschel, The Prophets (New York: Harper Collins, 2001).

13   N.T. Wright, "Jesus in the Perfect Storm," NTWrightPage.com, 2011, https://ntwrightpage.com/2016/03/30/jesus-in-the-perfect-storm/.

14   Matthew 21:10," σείω (seiō), σείομαι (seiomai): vb.; ≡ DBLHebr 8321; Str 4579; TDNT 7.196—1. LN 16.7 shake (Mt 27:51; Heb 12:26; Rev 6:13+); 2. LN 25.233 cause great anxiety (Mt 21:10+); 3. LN 16.6 (dep.) tremble (Mt 28:4+) Swanson, J. (1997). In

Dictionary of Biblical Languages with Semantic Domains: Greek (New Testament) (electronic ed.). Logos Research Systems, Inc.

15 "1544. Ekballo," Biblehub.com, 2021, https:// biblehub.com/greek/1544.htm.

16 Thomas Merton

17 Makoto Fujimura, Art and Faith: A Theology of Making (New Haven: Yale University Press, 2021), 31

18 Joe Spann, Tulsa Oklahoma

19 Makato Fujimura, Art and Faith: A Theology of Making (New Haven: Yale University Press, 2021), 4

20 Ian Cron, Chasing Francis (Grand Rapids: Zondervan, 2013), 223.

21 Christy Tennant, "Prophets, Artists, and Prophetic Artists," FullerStudio.com, 2022, fullerstudio.fuller.edu.

22 Strong's Concordance, "3365 Médamós," BibleHub. com, 2022, https://biblehub.com/greek/3365.htm.

23 Strong's Concordance, "3760 Oudamós," BibleHub. com, 2022, https://biblehub.com/greek/3760.htm.

24 LN 53.56 worship, bow as an act of allegiance or regard (Mt 2:2); 2. LN 17.21 prostrate oneself before, kneel down before as an act of reverence (Rev 3:9) Swanson, J. (1997). In Dictionary of Biblical Languages with Semantic Domains: Greek (New Testament) (electronic ed.). Logos Research Systems, Inc.

25 Diana R. Garland and Vicki Marsh Kabat, "Power and the Christian," Baylor.edu, 2009, https://www.baylor. edu/content/services/document.php/99706.pdf.

26 Sections of these notes were taken from Diana R. Garland and Vicki Marsh Kabat, "Power and the Christian," Baylor.edu, 2009, https:// www.baylor.edu/content/services/document.php/99706.pdf.

27 Martin Luther King, Jr., "Where Do We Go From Here?," address delivered at the 11th Annual SCLC Convention, Stanford Martin Luther King Jr. Research and Education Institute, 1967, https://kinginstitute.stanford.edu/king-papers/documents/where-do-we-go-here-address-delivered-eleventh-annual-sclc-convention.

28 James D. G. Dunn, Jesus and the Spirit: A Study of the Religious and Charismatic Experience of Jesus and the First Christians as Reflected in the New Testament (Kindle Location 4281).

29 "Fruits" would be the Fruit of the Spirit (see Galatians 5:22-23)

30 Wright, N. T.. Paul (p. 27). HarperOne. Kindle Edition

31 Abraham Heschel, The Prophets (New York: Harper Collins, 2001).

32 David Bosch, Transforming Mission: Paradigm Shifts in Theology of Mission (New York: Orbis, 2011).

33 Seth Kittinger, Akouo Missionary, Tulsa, OK

34 Seth Kittinger, Akouo Missionary, Tulsa, OK

35 Seth Kittinger, Akouo Missionary, Tulsa, OK

36 Seth Kittinger, Akouo Missionary, Tulsa, OK

Printed in Great Britain
by Amazon

42774527R00099